"Proven Systems to Free up Time for Digital Nomads, Non-Conformists, and Freedom Seekers"

Glen Kowalski

THE UNCONVENTIONAL ENTREPRENEUR

AUTOMATIC MARKETING SYSTEM

More Leads, Better Conversions, and Higher Customer Lifetime Value for Coaches, Authors, Speakers, Experts, Service Providers and other Freedom Loving Entrepreneurs - On Autopilot

Copyright 2017 All Rights Reserved

The Unconventional Entrepreneur Automatic Marketing System

MORE LEADS, BETTER CONVERSIONS, AND
HIGHER CUSTOMER LIFETIME VALUE FOR
COACHES, AUTHORS, SPEAKERS, EXPERTS,
SERVICE PROVIDERS AND OTHER
FREEDOM LOVING ENTREPRENEURS - ON
AUTOPILOT

Glen Kowalski

Palm Tree Publishing
Belize City, Belize

Copyright © 2017 Glen Kowalski

All rights reserved. No part of this publication may be reproduced, distributed, or transmitted in any form or by any means, including photocopying, recording, or other electronic or mechanical methods, without the prior written permission of the publisher, except in the case of brief quotations embodied in critical reviews and certain other noncommercial uses permitted by copyright law. For permission requests, write to the publisher, addressed "Attention: Permissions Coordinator," at the address below.

Palm Tree Marketing Group Ltd.,
2236 Albert Hoy Street,
Belize City, BZ 00000, Belize
www.GlenKowalski.com

Ordering Information:

Quantity sales. Special discounts are available on quantity purchases by corporations, associations, and others. For details, contact the publisher at the address above.

Printed in the United States of America

First Printing, 2017

ISBN-13: 978-1539501459

Contents

Introduction 1

    Who is an Unconventional Entrepreneur? 5

    Who this System is not for 6

    Who I Am 7

    The Guarantee 9

    Why Systemize and Automate 9

Introducing the Unconventional Entrepreneur Automatic Marketing System 15

    Why Automation? 16

Why do you do what you do? What drives you? 19

Audit 21

    Aim 23

    Tempt 24

    Capture Leads 24

    Amplification, Education, and Relationship Building 25

    Make an Offer 25

Close the Deal 26

Over Deliver and Wow 26

Offer More and Keep Your Clients Happy 27

Get Referrals and Go Viral 27

Completing the Audit 28

Action Steps 28

The Unconventional Entrepreneur Automatic Marketing System Audit 29

Target Your Customer 35

Market Place Sophistication 36

Whiteboard Exercise 37

Action Steps 43

Your Unique Selling Proposition 45

Action Steps 48

Marketing Automation Software 49

Infusionsoft 53

ActiveCampaign 56

Other Options 59

Action Steps 59

Sales Pipeline 61

Sales Pipeline or Marketing Funnel? 61

Why You Need a Pipeline (or Funnel) 64

What is Your Pipeline? 65

Why this is so Powerful 66

Action Steps 67

Attract More Clients with the Temptation Mechanism 73

Website / Platform 74

Creating Your Platform and Website 77

Action Steps 80

Identify Keywords or Problem Language Your Ideal Clients Use
 81

Identify Where Your Ideal Clients Are Hanging Out 83

Action Steps 84

Automation in the Attraction Process 84

Gaining Credibility 85

Seducing Your Ideal Clients 85

Action Steps 86

Capture Leads 87

    The Landing / Temptation Page 88

    Lead Magnet Ideas 89

    The Nuts and Bolts of your Temptation Page 92

    Landing Page Software 95

    Automating Your Lead Capture 96

    Double Opt In Confirmation 98

    Action Steps 101

Amplify Interest, Educate, Build Relationships 103

    Email Marketing - Auto-responders, Broadcasts, and more .. 105

    How to Write Email 112

    Be Creative and Personal 120

    Automating Email 121

Content Marketing Strategies 123

Make an Offer 129

    Types of Offers 129

    Back End Offers 134

What Is Your Offer 134

Launch Your Core Service 135

Close the Deal 137

Abandoned Carts 138

Sales Process 139

Over Deliver and Wow 145

Delivery 146

After Sales Service (The Wow Factor) 147

Action Steps 149

Loop Back and Offer More 151

Up Sells 152

Down Sells 153

Cross Sells 153

Subscriptions / Reoccurring Sales 154

Super Premium Products and Services 154

But What if You Don't Sell Other Products? 155

What if Your Prospects Don't Buy and or Go Cold? 156

The Loop Back Mechanism 159

Get Referrals 163

    Automatic Referral Program 165

    Product Launches and Events 168

    Joint Ventures and Other Partnerships 170

    Action Steps 171

Now, Get Out There and Do It 173

    More Help 174

Dedication

Dedicated to my wife Jinky Kowalski, an Unconventional Entrepreneur herself, for putting up with the many stops and starts this book has taken, and the many times I told her I was too busy to {Insert Anything Here} because I was writing.

Acknowledgments

I want to give special thanks to Tiffany Scott, my amazing branding coach, for helping to define the Unconventional Entrepreneur brand, her support, and for helping to hold my feet to the flames the many times I was ready to quit.
I also want to thank my proofreaders and beta readers for pointing out errors and places I could make improvements.
Finally, I want to thank my parents who have always supported me in anything that I've undertaken.

CHAPTER 1

Introduction

Congratulations, you're an unconventional Entrepreneur. My goal is that after reading this book, you'll be more excited about your entrepreneurial path, and never think of your business the same way. I'm so glad to meet you, there's so few non-conformists still bucking trends, stepping away from the 9 – 5, and fighting the good fight. As freedom seeking entrepreneurs, we're responsible for changing the world.

Maybe you're a coach, consultant, financial planner, investment professional, lawyer, real estate agent, info-marketer, radio or podcast hosts, or one of the other experts who are fighting the constraints of a 9 - 5 job. Whatever it is, you provide a service of some type. And in exchange you're looking for business and location independence. Later in this chapter we'll delve deeper into what independence means to you.

Regardless of what you call yourself, which is as individual as you are, you're an entrepreneur first. And as an entrepreneur, a few things are consistent.

First, you need a steady stream of new clients keeping your pipeline full, so you never have to worry about the feast or famine cycle so common in our line of work. And next, you want every client's lifetime customer value to be as high as possible so you know your family's well fed, and you'll be able to live a life of independence. Whatever that life of independence means to you.

You also want to provide the best results for your clients and have them raving to friends about the transformation you've made in their lives. Because regardless of what service you provide, ultimately that's what you're in the business of doing... Providing results and transformation.

There's one more truth about unconventional entrepreneurs universal for all of us. We only have 24 hours in a day and for almost everyone I work with, they'd rather provide services to their clients and change the world than handle the repetitive tasks involved in administration, sales, and marketing.

Plus, we'd prefer to spend time hours eating, sleeping, using the bathroom, and spending time with family, hobbies, or leisure. Since you're reading this book, I'll assume those hours never seem to be enough to get everything done your business needs to succeed in today's competitive world. It's a fact; today's entrepreneurs are busier than ever.

We need to be working on our business, transforming it into the freedom vehicle it should be. But instead, we're working in our business doing the same repetitive tasks, making the same revenue killing mistakes, and never seeming to get ahead or out of the normal day to day grind. I'm here to tell you it doesn't have to be this way.

In addition, marketing and sales are two of the most, I'd argue the most, important parts of your business. Yet they're usually areas of the business you'd rather avoid. You got into your business to provide your service, not because you want to spend all of your time finding those clients.

If you're like most of my clients, you'd be overjoyed if new clients chased you down, you worked with them longer, and they referred their friends. And all you had to do was provide results. You'd also prefer to never have to market your services, or sell anyone one about what you offer.

Am I right?

Unfortunately, we know that isn't the reality of your business. Instead, you have to hustle every day to find new clients if you want to reach your revenue goals or grow your business. And there's never enough time...

You know it takes more than a single flyer, advertisement, or web page to get someone to sign on the dotted line and become a client. And if you were like most service providers I talk to, you would prefer more of your clients and friends referring business your way?

One of the first questions I ask a prospective client is, "Are your closing rates, the number of clients you sign vs. the number of people you talk to, lower than you'd like to see?" Most times, the answer I get is a big fat "Yes." It might be the same for you.

Follow up failure is the biggest cause of lost revenues and low closing rates for service providers. In the past, experts told us it took 7 touch points, or contacts with a prospect, before they would buy from you. Today, thanks to the Internet and increased competition and skepticism, that number is closer to 18, but varies based on the industry.

Yet, businesses today, lose up to 80% of potential deals from this one reason. Follow up failure. What would an extra 80% of closed deals mean to your bottom line? For most businesses this one point alone could mean 6 or 7 figures difference in your business this year.

Are your sales team following up with your prospects 18 times or more? You might wonder who has time for that, right?

Fortunately, the Unconventional Entrepreneur Automatic Marketing System outlined in this book almost eliminates follow up failure, on autopilot. And what it can't automate, it will notify and kick the ass of someone who needs to get it done. But that's barely scraping the surface of the differences you'll see over the next 12 months if you follow the steps I've laid out.

Actually, it's better than that. I use the time frame 12 months because that's how long it takes to implement and optimize the entire system. But if you follow the steps, you'll see results right away. Every step in the system gives you either a fast leg up on your competition, or critical insights that help you set those pieces in place.

Using this system gets results throughout your entire customer lifecycle, making a large impact in multiple areas that turns into colossal changes for your business. When I work with private clients, I'll only take you on if I sincerely believe we can at least double your revenues within 12 months of the full system implementation. It's that powerful.

What would doubling your revenues over the next 12 months mean to you and your business? How would it change your life?

This is the life impacting change I want to help you make. If your business isn't automated now, and if you're not following a predictable, scalable, proven, and repeatable system (most businesses aren't) this transformation is possible. And faster than you might imagine.

Let's begin this journey now with a discussion about your business and the marketing systems and processes you follow today.

Who is an Unconventional Entrepreneur?

This system was created for unconventional entrepreneurs who care about their clients, and want to have more time to work on their business, instead of in their business. They want to do what they are passionate about, and spend more time on leisure, hobbies, or whatever they want to pursue inside and outside their work lives. All while pulling in more income, working with clients they love and want to work with, and building a strong brand and referral network.

By unconventional entrepreneur, I mean business owners who are fed up and refuse to live life in a conventional way. They abhor the conformist life of commuting through traffic, working a 9 - 5 job, getting home to watch some crappy sitcom or reality show, repeating it 50 weeks of the year, taking 2 weeks vacation, and repeating over and over again for 40 years. Then praying they'll live long enough to retire at 65 so they can start enjoying life.

Chances are you're a non-conformist, a rebel, or you just want to stand out and make an impact.

Your field might be in alternative investments like precious metals or international real estate, Bitcoin or crypto-currency, libertarianism / anarchy, offshore banking / investments, holistic or natural medicine, freedom / sovereignty, living abroad, or other non-mainstream specialty.

Or you might have a more mainstream domain, but you are (or want to be) a digital nomad, or someone who wants the freedom and independence to live and work anywhere in the world.

You could be a consultant, coach, lawyer, accountant, financial planner, alternative medical practitioner, real estate agent, online educator, info-marketer, radio or podcast host, speaker, or other expert. But the key thing that makes you "you" is you want to take full responsibility for your own life and choices.

This system will work for anyone who wants total business, life, and location independence.

Who this System is not for

The *Unconventional Entrepreneur Automatic Marketing System* is designed to take proven online marketing tactics, turn them into a scalable process, and then automate repetitive tasks, notify action required during critical milestones, wow your customers by going the extra mile, increase lifetime customer value, and get referrals from raving fans.

Implementation requires creating and following set processes and polishing those systems to make them efficient as possible. And it requires work (in some cases working your ass off). So if you aren't prepared to put in the front-end work, this isn't going to help you.

If you're the type of person who wants to continue marketing like it was done 20 years ago, or is unwilling to follow a proven system, you're not going to see the results you want.

You may still get some boost by implementing some of the individual tactics we talk about throughout the system. But without integrating the individual components into a full marketing strategy, and automating those steps, you aren't going to experience the transformation possible in your service business.

Who I Am

This book is about you and your business; it's not about me. But I think it'll help to have a short introduction.

My name is Glen Kowalski, and I am the founder of Palm Tree Marketing Group Ltd.

I am driven to help non-conformists' committed to taking action and responsibility over their own lives. This includes freedom seekers who never want to be reliant on government, a boss, or anyone else to dictate how or where they live their lives or run their businesses.

I started my first company at age 17 when I bought a failing beach kiosk business and turned it around and expanded into two successful locations in one summer. With a passion for technology I joined the Canadian Military and then went on and explored the world of corporate enterprise, working for Microsoft as a Software Design Engineer, among other technical roles. However, forever a freedom seeker, I'm again living the Unconventional Entrepreneur Lifestyle in Panama where I swim in the ocean daily and help clients build independent lifestyles.

I help my clients, independence-seeking entrepreneurs, create online highly converting automatic sales and marketing systems.

Primarily, this includes info-marketers, radio / podcast hosts, experts, writers, speakers, service professionals like coaches and consultants, and others in non-mainstream fields like alternative investments, liberty focused businesses, and digital nomads.

I'm an online marketing consultant who has worked with small and large businesses throughout my career.

However, it was growing up in a small business family that gave me my passion for you, the entrepreneur who loves and cares for his clients and is willing to do anything to help them get the results they desire... A trait I both admire and share.

Growing up, I saw my parents struggle with never having enough clients or time to grow their business the way they wanted to while still leaving time to live the life they wanted live. I know small business owners struggle to find balance between business growth and freedom. And it's my goal to help you get them both back.

My mission is awakening people to the availability of personal, location, business, and financial independence and serving those who are drawn to the unconventional.

And my vision is all people embracing their own independence and not bowing to the master of convention.

I've dedicated my life to learning, working with, and staying up to date on the latest online marketing strategies, and more importantly implementing them as part of a proven system and helping your small business succeed. This system will work for you if you work it. But I can't do it for you through this book. You have to step up, take responsibility, and take the steps you need to succeed. But as an Unconventional Entrepreneur, I know you're up to the challenge.

Even my private clients have work to do, since you and I aren't working together at the moment, you have a bunch more.

The Guarantee

Look, I'm required to tell you that any specific results we mention in the Unconventional Entrepreneur Automatic Marketing System book are not typical.

I don't know what your service is, or how much you charge. More importantly, I don't know if you'll read this book and hope that results will come to you without actually implementing the strategies.

Putting it under your pillow and hoping to absorb its content and implementation through osmosis is guaranteed to fail. For anyone using that strategy, sorry to ruin your day....

But I'll tell you this, if you're currently flying by the seat of your pants, or if you have a successful business, but your marketing isn't following an automated system like this one... You'll see a massive shift in your leads, sales, lifetime customer value, and referrals. And if you don't, I want to hear from you and see what we can do to get you back on track.

Maybe you need a little more coaching or accountability. Or maybe you'll want someone to build the entire system for you. But either way, and whatever it takes, if you are an unconventional entrepreneur, dedicated to your personal independence, I am committed to doing anything I can do to help you live your dreams the way you want and on your terms.

Why Systemize and Automate

When I was 19 years old, I remember standing in my barrack's bathroom with bloody knuckles and bloodshot eyes making a critical decision that would change my military career, and probably the rest of my life.

Ten minutes earlier, I'd been standing at attention in front of my short but stocky Master Corporal being berated and told I had failed my week's assessment in Basic Training. I already knew failing twice meant going back to the start of the 10-week program. And getting punted out of the military entirely wasn't far behind.

If you don't know, basic military training is several weeks of physiological, physical, and mental abuse meant to break you down and turn you into a soldier. The last thing you wanted was to start over, not to mention the self esteem kick to the nuts you'd feel seeing all your platoon mates graduate before you.

Anyway it turns out I failed that week due to a lack of attention to detail. To be specific, we had these little cards with our name and serial number on them and every morning we had to place those cards on our pillow for inspection. Being the young idiot new recruit I was, one morning, I had put it on my pillow upside down.

This may not sound important, but, as my Master Corporal told me through his perfectly manicured handlebar moustache, "Imagine being on a battlefield, field stripping a rifle, missing one crucial step, and getting shot in the head because your weapon jams."

Details matter.

After my review, I walked past my platoon, directly into the lime green washroom and into an empty stall.

Luckily for me, no one was around. It smelled like someone had been there recently, but that's for another story.

I stared up at the florescent lights, listened to them hum, and I'm embarrassed to say, broke down completely. In my defense, after 4 or 5 weeks of abuse, we were all feeling a little unbalanced.

As I stood there thinking about what my master corporal told me, my tears turned to rage, and I punched the concrete wall. Hard. Not hard enough to break anything, but hard enough to bleed, hurt, and get my composure.

Standing there, in an ugly, smelly toilet stall, I made a decision.

I would never let something so simple slip through the cracks again. I was going to create systems and processes. Everyday for the rest of basic training, and the rest of my career, I created checklists to follow to make sure every important detail was hit. Every time.

I finished out the rest of my basic training without failing again, and went on to excel as top student through the rest of my training.

I don't say that to brag, but to prove the value of systems and processes in almost everything we do.

Details matter. And its systems that allow you to follow processes in your business that are proven to be successful time after time.

Have you ever wondered why a McDonalds' Franchise sells for millions of dollars, or why someone would open a Taco Time, instead of just any old Taco stand (probably selling better tacos)?

Yes, brand recognition is important, but there's more to it than that. Brand recognition is a piece, but the brand recognition wouldn't exist if not for the systems and processes.

When you buy a franchise, you are paying for those proven systems and processes. These systems are specific steps in precise areas of the business that get a known result.

Wikipedia describes a system as...

> *A system is a set of interacting or interdependent component parts forming a complex/intricate whole. Every sys-*

tem is delineated by its spatial and temporal boundaries, surrounded and influenced by its environment, described by its structure and purpose and expressed in its functioning.

The term system may also refer to a set of rules that governs structure or behavior. Alternatively, and usually in the context of complex social systems, the term is used to describe the set of rules that govern structure or behavior.

In marketing and sales, a system is vital because it allows you to measure and then fine-tune results. Without systems in your marketing, you're taking shots in the dark and likely throwing away your marketing dollars. Let's look at a quick scenario.

For example, let's say you have a service selling for $100. If you're a graphic designer, this could be a Facebook timeline cover. Maybe it is an online course. Or 1 hour of consulting time. The number itself doesn't matter and is only used for illustrative purposes, it could be $1,000, $10,0000, or $1 million.

Anyway, that $100 is what one client is worth to your business.

You're running ads, putting up your webpage, handing out brochures, having shows, or whatever you do to make sales. But you have no idea what your return on investment (ROI) is. What do you do when your car breaks down or your water heater breaks? For whatever reason, if you suddenly need another $1,000, you have no idea what you need to do to get it.

If on the other hand, your marketing is systemized, this crisis is easily solved. Let's say your marketing system has 3 steps -- A, B, and C.

You know, if you do A, B, and C, it costs you $10 to get a lead, because your system has allowed you to measure your results.

You also know, once again because you have a process, you need 5 leads to make one sale. So you know it costs you $50 to get a $100 customer. If you need $1,000 right now, you now know you need to invest $1,000 in your A, B, C System to recover your investment plus get enough extra to cover your $1,000 emergency.

NC = Number of Customers

RC = Revenue Per Customer

CPC = Cost Per Customer Acquisition

(NC x RC) – (NC x CPC) = Revenue

This is an oversimplified example, but demonstrates how measuring results lets you plan your strategy for the future. Measuring results is meaningless without a repeatable marketing system.

Now consider, what if, you were able to reduce the cost of acquiring a customer? Or you're able to increase the profit, or customer lifetime value (CLV)?

How does that change the equation?

CHAPTER 2

Introducing the Unconventional Entrepreneur Automatic Marketing System

That's the first goal of the *Unconventional Entrepreneur Automatic Marketing System* -- to increase your lead count. Specifically we'll do this with the Unconventional Entrepreneur Attraction Process. You can sign up for a free webinar that teaches how to do this with webinars step by step at http://glenkowalski.com/webcast.

The next goals are amplifying interest in your leads so more of them turn into customers, and finally increasing their Customer Lifetime Value (CLV). Each of these 3 areas will have a profound effect on your bottom line.

Remember, there are only 3 ways to grow your business.
1. Increase the number of leads coming to your business.
2. Convert more leads into customers.
3. Increase the value, or amount each customer spends, of each client you deal with.

The *Unconventional Entrepreneur Automatic Marketing System* is focused on each of these areas, and by the time you've finished this book, you'll understand how to optimize each of these revenue-enhancing areas.

Why Automation?

But what if you could do all three while spending less, or even no day-to-day effort working on each of those areas? So your increase in revenues happens automatically in the background?

Automation is the keystone in the Unconventional Entrepreneur Automatic Marketing System, and the most important piece in increasing your free time while creating more revenues.

In my opinion, automation is just as important as having the system implemented at all. Because the truth is, while you could increase revenues using the system and not the automation, eventually you'd burn out.

Plus by adding the automation, your results will be more predictable, and more importantly they'll be scalable because it enables you to work on your business instead of in your business.

This system is traceable, scalable, and repeatable. And thanks to automation, once it's implemented, it runs almost on autopilot.

Once in place, you'll free up your time to grow your business, spend time doing the things you want to do, and be able to plot a consistent path towards the freedom you desire.

In addition, you'll raise revenues in a predictable way that doesn't result in burn out, missed calls, or follow up opportunities.

And most importantly, you'll be in a position to give your clients the attention and service they require, while wowing them every step of the way. Giving you a tribe of raving fans who can't wait to spend more money and tell their friends and colleagues to work with you and experience the result you provide for them.

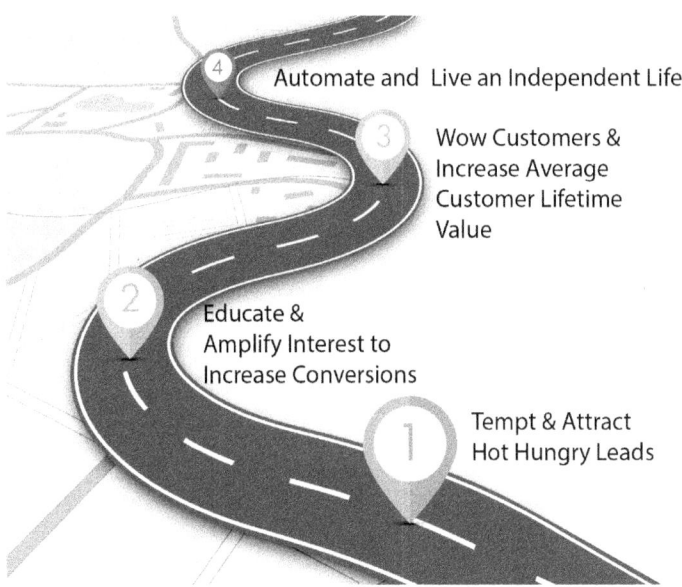

CHAPTER 3

Why do you do what you do? What drives you?

Like anything else in your business, the work of systemizing and automating comes down to priorities. Most of us get too involved with working in our businesses to work on our business. There always seems to be too many tasks and not enough time to do them.

Implementing automated systems are no different, and we both know that if you don't have a strong enough "why" you're not going to get around to implementing all the steps in this plan. So we are going to nip that in the bud right now before we get started.

Today's action step is easy, but it will help you gain clarity on where you want to go in your business. It will be a critical step as we progress through the system in the book.

1. How do you see your ideal business operating 1 year from now. Where are you spending your most time?

2. What does your business look like today? How many leads are you bringing in? How much time do you spend on day-to-day marketing and administrative tasks? How are your sales?

3. What do you see as the obstacles keeping you where you are to day compared to where you want to be? Will an automatic system that brings you more leads, turns more of those leads into sales, and increases the lifetime value of your customers help close that gap?

CHAPTER 4

Audit

"You can't know where you're going, if you don't know where you've been."

I don't know the origins of this quote, but Will Smith's Character said something similar in Hitch.

A more common quote is by Yogi Berra "If you don't know where you're going, any road will get you there."

We'll cover that more in the next chapter. But for now, we want to take a look at your current marketing. Specifically, the marketing you're currently doing, and where future opportunities are available.

By knowing what opportunities are available, it becomes a simple process to prioritize different strategies at appropriate places and as part of a system, instead of throwing crap against the wall and hoping some of it sticks.

Going through the audit accomplishes 2 essential goals.

1. It opens your eyes to many of the opportunities you may miss for increasing your leads and sales.

2. It lets us know what marketing tactics you're currently using and where you stand so we can make a solid plan.

It's impossible to build any process or system without a plan. And it is impossible to build a plan if you don't know 2 points. Where you're coming from, and where you want to end up.

In the last chapter, we established your "end goal" and we know creating more leads, turning more leads into sales, and increasing the lifetime value of every customer we service will help get us there. And in the next chapter we'll create our plan. Our map of how we'll get there.

You also identified where your business currently stood. This step is a more detailed view of how your current marketing plan fits into the current state of your business.

Every map, if it's going to be useful, has a starting point. Like when you are stuck in that infinite labyrinth known as a mall, and your significant other wants to shop in some obscure boutique but can't remember where it is. You walk up to the big machine at the door, type in the endpoint, and a big arrow pops up saying "You Are Here" with a map to get you to your location.

The *Unconventional Entrepreneur Automatic Marketing System Audit* determines your starting point and only takes a few minutes to complete. Within 30 minutes or less, you'll have a big arrow pointing at the "You Are Here" of your current marketing state.

Depending on the audit, your roadmap might include tying little pieces together into a system and getting them automated. Or, it may mean plotting the entire system from scratch in one or more focus areas. There's no way to know until you're done, so don't be tempted to skip this step. This is one of those "95% of business owners don't do this" points that could differentiate between success and failure.

We'll go into greater detail of the various parts of the system in future chapters but the audit is broken down into sections that correspond to the main areas your success system follows. The questions are straightforward and just identify individual tactics in the system, but not how they all fit together. We'll get to that later.

Remember the goal of the audit isn't to get a specific score; it's being honest with yourself so you know the opportunities ahead. The more unchecked boxes you have, the greater your opportunities for massive growth, so you should be excited for the future. Also, if you don't know the answer to a question, leave it unchecked for now since if you don't know the answer, we must refine it to fit into the system, anyway.

The audit covers 10 critical areas, all of which we'll discuss in more details as you progress through this workbook.

Aim

The key to any successful marketing campaign is knowing your customer. Many, if not most, businesses have never taken the time to figure that out. If you haven't, fear not, we'll be tackling that soon enough. Just check "No" to that question.

If you have, congratulations.

This section of the audit also asks if you've identified keywords. Keywords are critical in online advertising because it allows you to determine what words people use to find your business. We'll discuss keywords later in the book.

In addition, this section asks about your Unique Selling Proposition. Just answer the question honestly.

Tempt

This section covers what you're currently doing to attract new leads. There are 3 ways to increase the revenues in your business.

1. Get More Leads
2. Covert More Leads into Sales
3. Sell to your customer for higher amounts and more often.

The Unconventional Entrepreneur Automatic Marketing System covers all three, but the temptation / attraction process focuses on number one -- getting more leads into your funnel so you can create more customers.

It asks questions about your current advertising, traffic systems (like SEO), inbound marketing strategy, and more.

Capture Leads

This is the fun part, getting new leads into your funnel. 80% - 90% of websites are terrible for lead generation. Many website owners report paid traffic doesn't work. I'm telling you, the problem isn't the traffic, the problem is the website isn't optimized for lead conversion.

If yours isn't, that's great news, just think of the opportunities you have to skyrocket your business once we drill down on that area and turn your website into a lead machine.

The capture lead section of the audit form also has questions about your CRM. If there's any question you don't understand, just answer "No" and we'll get to it in the following chapters.

Amplification, Education, and Relationship Building

Customers are more sophisticated than ever, and they're also more skeptical. But even in the good old days it was rare you'd find a prospect that didn't know, like and trust you who'd drop several hundred dollars on your service; especially in an unconventional business like yours.

Sometimes moving a lead into a customer can be done quickly, but often it takes a longer period to go from lead to sale.

Did you know somewhere between 50% - 98% of leads visiting your website aren't ready to buy today? But a significant portion of those will buy over time if you keep nurturing them. Unfortunately, the opposite is also true. According to Marketing Sherpa, 79% of your leads will never buy, and lack of relationship building is cited as a major cause.

On the other end of the spectrum, companies that do a great job in the relationship area can increase sales by 50% at 33% less cost, according to automation leader, Marketo. The Annuitas Group reports nurtured leads make 47% larger purchases.

Make an Offer

Finally, our audit gets down to brass tacks, offering our new leads something of value in exchange for money. Diving down on what your offer is can be the most important step you take in your business. Bad copy with an awesome offer will sell like hotcakes.

However, you could have the best copy in the world, but if your offer stinks, sales will be poor, and refunds will skyrocket.

You most likely already have an offer, but answer the questions in this section with either a yes or no answer to identify any opportunities for what that offer is, or how it is presented.

Close the Deal

This section of the audit asks questions about how you collect payment for you offers. It might seem obvious and an oversight (for many companies it is), but how you collect your payment can make a big difference in your time, record keeping, and the amount of effort you spend working "in" your business. I've noticed many coaches don't accept credit cards up front, or have many other roadblocks to accepting money.

This can have a direct impact on revenue because having the wrong payment systems can increase cart abandonment, cost you more in transaction fees, or introduce other problems like your prospect changing their minds between talking to you and making a wire transfer.

Also, as part of your overall Unconventional Entrepreneur Automatic Marketing System, how this area is handled will affect other parts of the system since it is all a well-oiled machine.

Over Deliver and Wow

Notice I didn't just say deliver. I said **over deliver**. *The Unconventional Entrepreneur Automatic Marketing System* assumes you already have an awesome service, and that you deliver on it in a way that satisfies your customers.

But you don't just want your customers satisfied, you want them ecstatic raving fans.

This section of the audit covers your delivery system, and how you get your service, information, or product to your customers.

Eventually, your goal will be to make this process wow worthy, and automatic so you save time and effort for growing your business.

Offer More and Keep Your Clients Happy

Remember earlier we said one way to earn more income was to sell more often and for higher prices? This part of the audit asks specific questions to see how your existing marketing is working in that department.

Many companies focus all of their effort on getting new clients, making a sale, and then repeating that process. They completely ignore their existing customers as a source of new business. This massive mistake can cost your company thousands.

Once you've implemented, and continue implementing, *The Unconventional Entrepreneur Automatic Marketing System*, you'll never leave this massive source of revenues on the table again. If you've over delivered on your last promise, don't you think you owe your existing clients the opportunity to work with you again to solve more of their problems?

Of course you do.

Get Referrals and Go Viral

Your customers love your service. You've helped them solve their problems and they want to return the favor, and to help their friends too. But sometimes, they don't know how, or need a little push.

What are you doing today to foster referral relationships with your customers and other businesses in your industry? Are there any areas that could be approved upon?

You'll know once you complete this last section of the audit.

Completing the Audit

That's all there is too it. Answer a few questions, and you'll identify the holes in your current marketing processes and tactics.

But remember, there's more to *The Unconventional Entrepreneur Automatic Marketing System* than just checking "Yes" for these questions. Many entrepreneurs buy the next shiny object marketing product and implement it with no thought how all the tactics work together in a system.

Remember, its systems and processes that are the key to successfully growing your business on autopilot. And a few well-connected tactics as part of an automated system will take you much further than implementing every marketing tactic available without a strategy for making the parts work together.

Now that you know where you are, and you've dropped the "You are Here" arrow on your map, its time to plot the path to your end goal... happy high value clients. But to do that, we need to know who those happy clients are, and what they want more than anything else in the world.

In the next chapter, we'll get to work identifying that client, and planning the system we need to reach them exactly where they need you to be.

Action Steps

Action Step 1. Perform Your Audit Now

The Unconventional Entrepreneur Automatic Marketing System Audit

Directions

Use this easy 9 Point Marketing Audit & Checklist to identify holes in your marketing plan, or areas where you could do better. Simply answer each question as objectively as possible. Remember, the goal is to increase the profitability of your marketing. It's not to "get the right score". Nor is it about ego. Answer honestly and you're guaranteed to find areas of improvement for your website and other online marketing strategies.

NOTE: If you do not understand something or if you're not sure about your answer then please check "No"

Reflect

Objective	Yes	No
Have you completed the Marketing Automation Success System audit (Step 1 of the system)?	☐	☐
If no, the audit is below. Please complete it, and then follow the instructions at the end of the audit for step 2.		

Take Aim

Objective	Yes	No
Have you made a customer avatar describing your perfect client	☐	☐
Have you identified a list of 5 – 10 Keywords for your business	☐	☐

Have you identified your company's USP (Unique Selling Proposition) and how it relates to your customer avatar?	☐	☐

Magnetize Your Business

Objective	Yes	No
Does your website clearly convey your company's USP (Unique Selling Proposition)?	☐	☐
Do you have an Explainer video on your home page?	☐	☐
Do you utilize separate landing pages for specific products and services?	☐	☐
Have you identified where your ideal customers are spending their time online and offline?	☐	☐
Are you engaging your potential clients in those places?	☐	☐
Do you have a paid traffic strategy in place?	☐	☐
If Yes to previous question, are you running and testing various ads	☐	☐
Are you sending paid traffic to different landing pages that match the message and tone of your advertisements?	☐	☐
Are you setting Facebook tokens on website visitors so you can send them targeted advertising you know they'll find interesting?	☐	☐
Are you running retargeting campaigns to non-lead visitors to move them down your marketing funnel?	☐	☐
Are you a published author? Meaning have you published a print book for credibility and authority in your marketplace?	☐	☐
Is your website mobile friendly and optimized?	☐	☐
Have you tested Facebook, Google, LinkedIn, YouTube, and other paid traffic channels?	☐	☐
Is your website optimized for SEO?	☐	☐
Do you have a presence in social media?	☐	☐
Are you updating it regularly?	☐	☐
Do you have a company blog?	☐	☐
Are you updating it at least once a week with new and engaging content?	☐	☐

Capture Leads

Objective	Yes	No
Do you have an optin form to capture email addresses?	☐	☐
Are you giving something valuable (information, products, tools, etc.) in exchange for a visitors email address?	☐	☐
Are your sales reps being automatically notified when a new lead enters the system?	☐	☐
Are you testing various lead attraction items to find the one that resonates most with your audience?	☐	☐
Have you tested headlines, copy, colors, images, and other aspects of your landing pages in order to get the best conversion?	☐	☐
Do you have a mechanism in place to do so?	☐	☐
Are you automatically adding your leads to a customer relationship manager (CRM)	☐	☐
Can you view all your leads contact details, email history, score, purchase history, etc. at a glance?	☐	☐

Educate and Build Relationships

Objective	Yes	No
Do you send automated follow emails to build the relationships?	☐	☐
Do you have a YouTube channel?	☐	☐
On your YouTube channel do you create short but valuable "Education Based" videos to help your target market make a good buying decision?	☐	☐
Do you send out broadcast emails, text messages, Tweets and Facebook posts about special deals or events?	☐	☐
Do you have a content strategy that includes blog, e-books, webinars, teleseminars, etc.?	☐	☐
Do you issue press releases on a regular basis to introduce new products, services and other newsworthy topics?	☐	☐

Make an Offer

Objective	Yes	No
Do you have an automatic funnel tracking system that tells you the optimal time to make an offer?	☐	☐
Is your sales team spending the most time on the potential customers who are most ready to purchase?	☐	☐
Are you scoring your leads based on the actions they have taken?	☐	☐
Do you have one or more compelling offers based on the knowledge gained during the targeting and attraction phases.	☐	☐
Do you know when your ideal prospects are in the evaluation phase?	☐	☐
Have you tested the copy on your offer pages including headlines?	☐	☐
If you have an e-commerce site, or online sales, have you tested all aspects of your offers presentation?	☐	☐
Have you productized your knowledge into a revenue multiplying online course to showcase your knowledge, create a new revenue stream, and position yourself as an expert in your industry?	☐	☐
Have you completed a product launch of your flagship product or service?	☐	☐

Close the Deal

Objective	Yes	No
Do you have an easy method of invoicing and collecting payment?	☐	☐
Do you have consistent onboarding procedures for new clients to ensure they get off to a good start with your product or service?	☐	☐
Do you have clear and effective processes in place for closing the sale?	☐	☐
Are your sales reps trained in those procedures?	☐	☐
Do you have clear and professional documentation to demonstrate to your customer you have a well run, experienced organization?	☐	☐
Are your sales reps notified immediately of hot sales opportunities?	☐	☐

Over Deliver and Wow

Objective	Yes	No
Do you have an automated and / or repeatable process for delivering on time and on budget?	☐	☐
Do you have automated appointment setting, task creation, and tracking to ensure you never miss a meeting or deadline?	☐	☐
Do you automatically send thank you notes, gifts, and other items thanking and wowing your customers?	☐	☐
Do you create fulfillment lists for various products and services you sell?	☐	☐
Is that process automatic?	☐	☐
Are digital files automatically sent or downloadable after purchase?	☐	☐
Do you have a secure members area for clients to access products, reports, or other collateral?	☐	☐
Is that membership tied with your CRM, E-Commerce, and marketing software?	☐	☐
Do you provide after purchase service such as thank you cards, unique packaging, coupons, personal phone calls, tutorials, surveys, announcements, or birthday wishes?	☐	☐
Is that after sales service automatic and for every customer?	☐	☐

Offer More and Keep Your Clients Happy

Objective	Yes	No
Are you offering cross sells of other products to your customers either immediately, or down the line?	☐	☐
Are you offering an immediate upsell after purchase, later in the cycle, or both?	☐	☐
Are you notifying clients of new products or services?	☐	☐
Do you run time limited special promotions for customers only?	☐	☐
Do you market to former customers to bring them back?	☐	☐
Do you have an automated system that takes care of all of the above on autopilot?	☐	☐
Do you survey your customers to find out what they want most?	☐	☐

Get Referrals and Go Viral

Objective	Yes	No
Are you asking your clients for referrals from their friends and / or colleagues?	☐	☐
Do you offer a gift, discount, or other incentives like movie tickets for referrals?	☐	☐
Do you have a full-blown referral program?	☐	☐
Do you encourage good customers to leave online review on Yelp and Google?	☐	☐
Do you partner with other non-competing businesses to cross promote each other?	☐	☐
If you are a local business, do you have your business listed in the Top 15 Local Directories? Ex., Have you claimed your Google Local	☐	☐

CHAPTER 5

Target Your Customer

I know, you've heard it a million times... Well, dammit, you're going to hear it again.

Because, have you ever sat down and done it?

You need to figure out who your ideal client is, what their pain points are, and what they need.

I ask because most entrepreneurs I talk to haven't. Or they've only given it a halfhearted effort. I'm guilty of it. Almost everyone I know is guilty of it. And by far the majority of the clients I work with are guilty of it until we work together and finally get this defined. Everyone starts out hating the process, so they tend to ignore it. But if you follow the plan I've lain out below, you might even find it fun and start to enjoy it.

Face it, not everyone is a customer. Some people need it but won't want it... Some people want it but won't need it...

And others, you wouldn't want to work with if they stood vigil outside your office for 3 days with a mariachi band and a candle. Ok, yes, quite often we'll buckle to pressure and give that group service too. And while there are a million reasons that's a bad idea, we'll save that discussion for another book.

For now, let's look at who your ideal client is, and why its critical we know **who** we're marketing to.

By far, the most successful marketing copy, or the words you use in your advertising, is the copy that speaks directly to your clients. It's not enough to list your products benefits, features, or strengths. You need to speak in a language your prospect understands and bonds with. You need to point out their pain, and give them a clear path to the solution.

And you need to make them like you to want to do business with you.

Just like in personal relationships, not everyone will be your friend, and you won't sell to everyone. Your goal has to be to enter the conversation your ideal client is already having in their mind. How can you do that if you don't know who they are, and where they are hanging out?

Market Place Sophistication

Speaking of entering the conversation in your clients mind, knowing your client's market place sophistication is critical. Simply stated, you have to know and understand what marketing messages your clients have already been exposed to and seen in their market.

Without understanding what your clients have already seen, how can you possibly stand out and be different?

Quick answer... You can't.

Fortunately, knowing who your client is doesn't have to be difficult and can be kind of fun. It takes work and effort. But I guarantee if you take the time, and give it an honest effort you will find insights you never recognized before. And your marketing copy, whether it's on webpages, brochures, emails, or anywhere else, will be much stronger and more effective.

Its possible to outsource the front end of this work if you give your virtual assistant the right questions. I'll give you those in a moment. But you'll still have to organize and interprets the data for your business. And you might have to burn through a few VA's before you find one who can give you the level of quality you want.

I've had limited success with VA's and even employees, and think you'll be much more effective if you follow this three step approach as a team with everyone working together. Either way, you'll have to take the lead since it's your business.

Whiteboard Exercise

Step 1 – Who Your Idea Client is

To begin this exercise, start with a large white board and different colors of sticky notes. The more team members you gather together the better since you will all feed off each other's ideas as you start to brainstorm.

Grab a box of donuts, call everyone into the conference room, give them a pen, a stack of notes, and get to work.

Draw a big X, from the top corner to the other side about 3/4^{the} of the way down, on the white board with the intersection in the middle.
1. In the top section write "Thinks and Feels"
2. In the Left section write "Sees"
3. In the right section write "Hears"
4. In the bottom part of the X write "Does"

5. Then in the middle section on the left right "Pains" and on the right side "Gains".

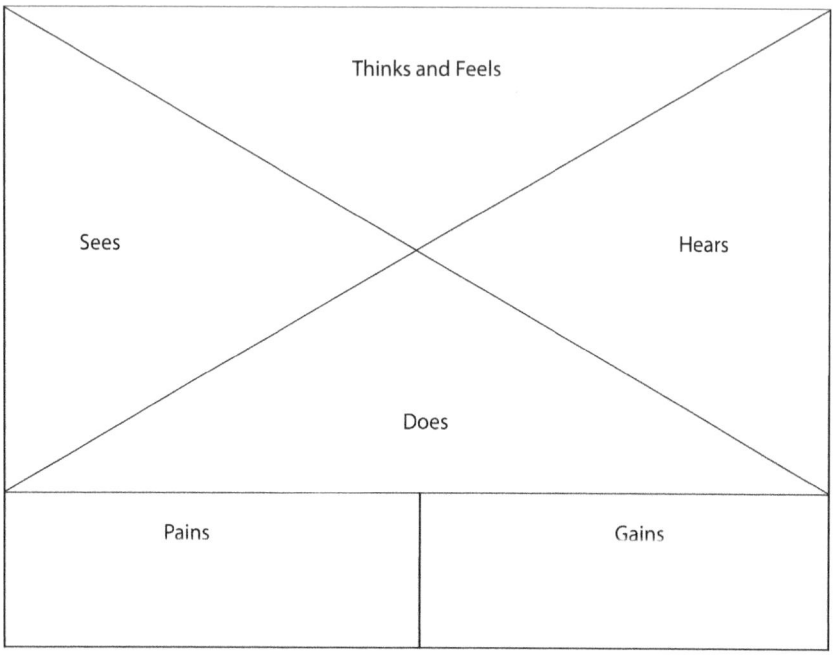

The goal of this exercise is to brain storm everything you think about who your ideal client is. Keep in mind you could have more than one ideal client, but you'll break out who those ideal clients are in the next step. For now, you want to let you imagination run wild and just get your thoughts out there.

Under <u>Thinks and Feels</u>, start placing sticky notes about what your ideal client is thinking about, for example.
- "I'm too fat."
- "At my age there's no more fun in life, everything seems said and done."
- "My business is in trouble."

- "My friends think I'm being a snob, but I have to work all the time or I'm going to lose my business."
- "I'm stressed out all the time."
- "The government won't stay out of my business."
- Etc.

What is your client thinking about right now. Ideally, most of what he is thinking about will be related to what your offer, but not everything, so don't limit yourself. One insight will lead to many others.

Under the <u>Sees</u> Section, list out what your ideal client sees during his / her day. For example...

- "Thin women on all the billboard signs."
- "Younger more energetic people having more fun."
- "Colleagues driving nice luxurious vehicles."
- "The Jones's up the street going on a family vacation."
- "Friends getting lawsuits, or experiencing confiscations."
- "Tax notices in the mail."

You get the idea.

Under the <u>Hear</u> section is very similar except deals with a different modality some people respond stronger too. This can include orders they get, what they hear on the radio, what their friends are telling them and more...

- "Don't wear this, wear that instead."
- "You'll never succeed in business"
- "If you want to automate your business, you need to start with knowing who your ideal client is."
- "You should quit this entrepreneur thing and get a real job."
- "You shouldn't travel there, they have exotic diseases."

And then the last section of the X is Does. This is what is your client telling other people, and actually showing through his or her actions.
- "I hate how I look in this dress."
- Heading to the bar every night and getting drunk - Action
- Stays late at the office and never sees his family - Action
- Has high levels of encryption setup on computers and electronics - Action

These sections should not be filled out in any particular order, but as the answers come to you. Spend as much time as you need.

Step 2 – Identify Pains and Gains

Once you've exhausted this vision of your ideal customer(s), you'll already begin seeing a picture emerge. I can guarantee you'll feel closer to your client than you've ever felt, and even have a picture in your mind as to what they look like, and how they live.

That's perfect, and exactly what you are going for. You might want to surf the internet looking for pictures until you find someone who matches what that customer looks like. And stick it right in the middle of the X.

So now you know who they are, what they see, what they're listening to, and what they do, you can move onto step 2 which is identifying your ideal clients pains and gains.

Everything that you might sell, from a stick of gum to a corporate jet or yacht satisfies one of two basic needs. Everyone buys to either move towards something. Or because they're moving away from something.

What they are moving towards, are the gains. Write those in the gains column of your whiteboard. This could be things like...
- Prestige or esteem

- Living abroad
- Comfort
- Luxury
- Better health or a sexier body
- Privacy
- Etc.

On the other side of the spectrum are pains. These are situations your ideal client is trying to move away from. As a general rule, people work harder trying to move away from things they don't want than they do trying to move towards things they do want. That's why you see so much negative advertising, especially in the financial services space.

There's an old story floating around, I think I heard it from Zig Ziglar the first time.

> *There was once a traveling salesman working the back roads of Iowa when he came upon an old farmer sitting on the porch beside an old hound dog. He walked up to the old man and introduced himself, when all of a sudden the dog let out an ungodly howl.*
>
> *The salesman, being a seasoned professional, tried to ignore the dog and went on with his pitch. But every few minutes more howling or crying interrupted him.*
>
> *Finally, the salesman asked, "What's wrong with your dog."*
>
> *"Oh him," the farmer replied. "He's just laying on a nail."*
>
> *"Well why doesn't he get up and move?"*

> *"Well, it hurts it bad enough for him to bitch about it, but not enough to actually do anything to change it."*

Many of our ideal clients are in that exact same position. They want to lose weight, increase their business success, or do whatever it is your service will do for them. But they don't want it bad enough to take action.

Your job is to understand what those pains are. And if you're going to "go negative" and advertise to those pains, make sure you "back up the hearse" and let them feel the pain before giving them the way out. Identify those pains, and magnify them as large as you can.

To do that successfully, you need to know what those pains are. Get out your sticky notes and place them on the board.

These could be things like...

- Fear of lawsuits
- Excessive taxation
- Lack of privacy.

Step 3 – Create Your Avatar(s)

Congratulations, you have a great picture of where your client is coming from, who they are, where they want to go, and how you're going to market to them. If you stopped here, you would already be miles ahead of your competition.

But there's still one more step you'll want to take, which is to organize, prioritize, and analyze your data.

How you do that doesn't matter. We have an internal format we use with our clients, but as long as the information is noted down somewhere that's what's important.

Based on the picture you currently have of your client(s) you want to identify personas or avatars. An avatar is just a picture of your client you can use in your mind whenever you do any marketing. It's most powerful if you give that person a name, and you can even go to Google images to find a picture of someone you think fits that description.

There are plenty of books and courses available on creating customer personas, so we won't go too much deeper into it as part of our system. But in a nutshell, you'll want to list:

- The pain and gain points you listed above.
- Each of the 4 segments you created with your sticky notes.
- Where that person you identified will hang out (social media, physical venues, etc.)
- Who that person listens to (guru's, media, magazines, TV)
- Their basic demographics - age, income, location, etc.
- Politics (if it's important to your niche - it is for most unconventional entrepreneurs.
- Any other insights you've gathered during this process.

Put all this information in a legible format and make sure your marketing, sales, and customer support staff have it available and close to them at all times. You should consider sticking this information right next to your monitor and telephone, as you'll want to refer to it every time you perform any type of marketing or sales communication.

Action Steps

Action Step 1. Draw a large copy of the above diagram on a whiteboard, gather your team and a stack of sticky notes, and identify at least one customer avatar.

Action Step 2. Gather and organize the information from your whiteboard into a comprehensive description of your ideal customer. Give your customer a name and find a picture that matches so whenever you are communicating with your client, either on the web, in print, or in person you can speak to one person. That ideal client.

CHAPTER 6

Your Unique Selling Proposition

Another concept every business owner has heard of, but most never do, is identify their Unique Selling Proposition. What is it that makes your business unique from all your competitors? Why would your customers buy from you, instead of them? Especially if you aren't the cheapest option on the block. By the way, Unconventional Entrepreneurs are never the cheapest option on the block.

In today's crowded market place, our prospects are more confused than ever as to where to spend their hard earned cash and where to place their trust. Sure, your awesome service offerings are exactly what they need, and should be able to differentiate you. But they're not. Your prospects don't know you yet, and if you don't capture their attention, and let them know what makes you different, they're just as likely to go to your competitor.

That would of course be a mistake for them, so it's your responsibility to identify and communicate what makes you different.

Reams of material have been written about creating your USP, and it is far from the main point of the Unconventional

Entrepreneur Automatic Marketing System. But because every component in the system involves some type of communication with your ideal clients, and every communication you have with your clients and potential clients should reflect your USP, it is critical that you have at least a basic framework.

I don't think you need to polish it until your fingers bleed or it's worded exactly like some corporate monologue - leave that to the conformists. I also don't think anyone other than you (and your marketing and sales teams) even need to see what you've come up with, because you'll be communicating it automatically with every marketing message you create.

If you don't have one now, start basic, you can always change it later. The most important part is taking action and getting clear in your head what makes you stand out in your market. So you can begin to convey whatever it is that you offer.

After you've figured out what your unique proposition is, grab your customer avatar - you have created one, right? If not, go back to the previous chapter.

You now have your selling proposition and your ideal client. Your assignment from now on, in every piece of marketing you do, and in every sales conversation, is to craft a message that makes you uniquely valuable to your ideal client.

However, your USP should do more than identify you to your ideal customers. It should dissuade clients who are not in your ideal demographic. In fact, you're a busy person, let's be honest, it should repel them. After all, if you aren't pissing somebody off, you probably don't have anything to say. And you certainly aren't unconventional.

For an extreme example, look at Abercrombie and Fitch. They've actively come out and said they will only market to the "cool" and beautiful people of the world. And they've actually gotten a huge backlash because of their insensitive marketing. That backlash hasn't affected their sales though, and has appeared to strengthen their brand.

Before you scream at me, I'm not advocating for Abercrombie &Fitch. I'm personally repulsed by their practices and refuse spend money on their over priced, socially conformist clothing. But I'm proving a point. I'm not their customer because I was never was part of the conventional "in" crowd they market to.

The moral of the story is, you don't want to waste your time on clients who are not a good fit for you. And you don't want those prospects wasting time with you if they can be better served elsewhere. So having a unique selling proposition that attracts ideal clients and lets non-ideal clients look elsewhere is the best win-win for everyone involved.

Your USP should be personal, honest, and unique. Remember, your goal is to enter the conversation your client is already having in their mind.

Crafting an effective selling proposition requires knowing your customers, knowing your industry, understanding what makes you different, and conveying those differences is a way that separates you from the rest. It's not enough to be the best. You need to be unique.

Because if everyone is competing to be the best, it becomes a crowded market place at the top.

List the features and benefits you offer, and find proof your ideal customers will understand and respect.

Then, take all that information and condense it into 1 to 3 sentences, and you're done. You'll want to tweak your USP over time as you hone in on your ideal customers and services. But for now, that's enough. You don't want to get trapped in a situation where you're messing with your USP for months on end, and procrastinating actually going to market.

Get something done today, even if its the down and dirty version at first. It's critical to have one, but it doesn't have to be perfect before you start the rest of the system.

With a USP, you want to be different. Pick your niche and craft a unique selling proposition that tells your ideal customers who you are, and how you can help, in a way no one else in your market can.

Action Steps

Action Step: Craft your ideal Unique Selling Proposition Now.

CHAPTER 7

Marketing Automation Software

One of the first questions someone might ask after completing a discovery session and putting together a marketing plan is, "Can I get started with this system without purchasing any software."

And the answer, is "Yes and No. And then no again."

The Unconventional Entrepreneur Automatic Marketing System is a step-by-step process for gathering more leads, wowing your customers, and increasing their lifetime value by marketing the right way to the right leads at the right time.

And in that regard the system could be followed without purchasing a single lick of software. You could get more leads, wow them, and increase their lifetime value.

However, those results alone are not what we're looking to accomplish. The idea of the system, and the reason you'll want to follow it, is to make more revenues, and free up your time to grow your business or spend doing what you want. And that's why "Automatic" is called out in the title.

That's where the automation part comes in. And it's also why you need software, and you need it immediately after your plan is created, not several months or years down the line. Sure, it might be possible to start implementing the plan without the software in place. But here's what's going to happen...

1. You'll run yourself ragged trying to manually accomplish each step in the process. Sending mails, segmenting lists, wowing customers, following up on leads, sending content or gifts, etc. So, instead of freeing up your time, you'll be spending more time than ever working in instead of on your business. And you'll never get out of the trap because you won't have a chance to actually get the automation setup properly in the first place. You'll most likely burn out long before that.

2. Unless you're a world-class web developer, you'll spend thousands of dollars building pages, thank you pages, blog pages, membership sites, etc. And then you'll need to pay again to get them rebuilt with the automation system in place. So you'll be reducing your revenues instead of adding to them. And if you are a world-class web developer, see item number 1 above.

3. You'll eventually decide you need the automation and software and it'll not only cost what it would have cost to setup in the first place, you'll have added expenses trying to migrate all of your manual data and leads, campaigns, and more.

I call the process the *Unconventional Entrepreneur Automatic Marketing System* because automation is the anchor that holds the entire process together and lets your marketing continue and grow... Almost on autopilot.

The next thing I see quite often is the other end of the spectrum. In fact, this is an even more common approach to marketing automation, CRM implementation, and Internet marketing in general.

It's the person who thinks they can buy a piece of push button automation software (or software of any type), and not have a strategy behind implementing and using that software.

I don't know what the percentage is of automation, email marketing, or CRM users who go down this path. But I suspect its a majority, and explains why providers of these services need to keep marketing. If the software was utilized in a way that became part of the business processes, the users would never leave. And the software companies would have more business than they can handle.

Fortunately, you don't have to go down that road, because you're going in with a strategy in how you're going to use the software. And the software will be implemented as needed.

For the purposes of the Marketing Automation Success System, there are 3 core revenue areas that power the entire process. And then a couple of other pieces you may need along the way depending on your business.

These components will be tied together via tight integration and works together like a well-oiled machine. Not as a bunch of unrelated parts, which is how most businesses are run today. Many businesses today try to patch together various pieces of technology without a system. And then complain that none of the components work when they fail miserably.

The 3 core pieces of software that power the Unconventional Entrepreneur Automatic Marketing System are:

1. An Auto-responder. An Auto-responder is a service that allows you to send automatic follow-up mails, thousands of broadcast mails, newsletters, and more. Without an Auto-responder, you'd be forced to hand write every single email, and will likely get banned by your ISP for sending spam. We'll talk in more detail about why this is

critical in later chapters. Examples of Auto-responders include Infusionsoft, ActiveCampaign, AWeber, GetAResponse, and Constant Contact.

2. A Customer Relationship Manager (CRM). A CRM is the key to a successfully run sales organization of any type. It keeps track of your contacts, let's you know what leads are hot, allows you to wow your customers by giving post sale follow up support and more. Many sales reps bitch and complain about using a CRM, but that's because the companies who used them threw them at the sales staff without a proper system and process behind them. Examples of CRMs are SalesForce, Infusionsoft, ActiveCampaign, Insightly, Zoho CRM, and a host of others.

3. Marketing Automation Software. Yes, I know, big surprise, since the core of this system is automation. The automation software ties the CRM and Auto-responder together to make sure the right follow-up is done with the right contacts at the right time. It allows you to systemize your processes and eliminate the repetitive work in trying to gather leads, increase their lifetime value, and wow them every step of the way. As Infusionsoft likes to say, "Its the personal touch, without the personal time."

Two top marketing automation suites, in my opinion, are Infusionsoft and Active Campaign. You'll notice that's because they also showed up in all 3 groups. It's also because they reasonably priced and extremely powerful. These are the two systems you'll see examples of often in this book.

The great thing about automation software is, if you follow my recommendations, they include the auto-responder and CRM. Between the two, which one I recommend depends on your business, goals, and situation, but you can get started with either for much less than you might think.

In addition to the automation software I recommend, you'll also need tools to help you design webpages quickly, easily and cheaply, sell products and take payments online, and potentially other analytics.

For your landing pages, I recommend OptimizePress, Lead Pages, or Click Funnels. For taking payments, it depends a lot on your business. WooCommerce though is great for many applications, and Infusionsoft has payment processing built in.

Finally, because a big system you'll hear about later, is Webinars. You'll need software to handle that, like Easy Webinar, Webinar Jam, EverWebinar, or WebinarJEO. But only if you want to use Webinars, and we have a separate free training for that if you are interested.

But first, to answer the question we opened up the chapter with, yes, you could try implementing the system without software. But you'll need to write your own (very costly), you're not going to get the results you want, and you're going to burn out. And if you follow along, the costs and risks are so low, you'll wonder why anyone would even try.

Infusionsoft

Infusionsoft currently claims to be the most popular automation suite in the world for small businesses. At the time of this writing they power the automation requirements of around 30,000 businesses.

They earned their strong reputation in the marketing automation space by creating an all in one tool that combines marketing automation, CRM, Auto-responder, E-commerce, landing pages and more.

And they've done it at a price small businesses can afford.

Other options, like Marketo, might have a few more bells and whistles built in. But they come at a cost of thousands of dollars a month.

You can get into Infusionsoft starting at $199 per month, and going up from there.

And if you need more, they have a colossal marketplace of technical partners who have built every type of add on your business could ever require.

One click up sells, no problem. Deeper analytics, yep. Affiliate tracking, no problem.

Of course everyone of these features comes at a cost. But at least you can add them when they're needed, and not be forced to take them if you don't.

Advantages

- All components work together out of the box because they're all built as part of the same platform.
- Includes CRM, Automation, E-commerce, Landing Pages, Optin Forms, Etc., all integrated together right out of the box.
- Massive network of consultants and developers so it's easy to get anything you need done at any time.
- Consistent branding throughout the tool as an advantage to you, and in your marketing materials.
- Ability to tag contacts with information for segmentation.
- Huge library of documentation, how to videos, marketing support, and more.

- 24 / 7 tech support.
- Excellent email deliverability. I think this is because the cost keeps a lot of spammers out of the system.
- Integration with a wide variety of 3rd party add ins.
- Hundreds of different training reports and videos available on marketing, sales, email and much more.
- Excellent duplicate record clean up.
- Powerful sales team and access control management.

Disadvantages

- $1999 and up required kick start fee. I hesitated putting this as a disadvantage. I think the kick-start fee is a great idea since it ensures you actually use the system the right way. But it is a high-risk proposition for some very small businesses since it doesn't allow you to try the software first. I recommend working with a consultant to ensure you get the full value.
- The $199 - $499 per month cost immediately out of the gate can be difficult for some small businesses who are new to the power of online marketing and / or marketing automation. It can be worth it in the end, but it is a big bite to chew.
- Steep learning curve. I have a number of clients who complain about the difficulty in navigating their way around the software. Part of this difficulty is due to its power and complexity, but many tasks could be made easier.
- Built in E-Commerce platform is far from best in breed. It's great the e-commerce is built in, and has seamless

integration. But it can be confusing and the customization options leave a lot to be desired.
- Users need fluency in English to use the tool, other languages are not supported. Since I have Spanish speaking clients, this was one big reason I started looking for options outside of Infusionsoft, but its not a big deal if you are US based and / or English speaking.
- Email templates are not mobile responsive (note: at writing time they have a beta version of mail that will be).
- No custom branding in domain name for cart, thank you pages, shopping pages, landing pages, etc.

Overall, Infusionsoft is a wonderfully powerful tool. I consult on Infusionsoft, have used it for many years, and I absolutely love the power of the system. The ideal demographic for Infusionsoft has over $250,000 / year in revenues, a sales team of 5 - 25 people, and spends several thousand dollars per month on marketing.

You should plan on having an Infusionsoft consultant on retainer for as long as you use this system.

You can watch some great videos and get more information and a demo here.

ActiveCampaign

ActiveCampaign is making a huge impact in the automation market, and Infusionsoft users and consultants are flocking towards this amazing automation suite in droves. Right now, it is the most common solution I recommend to my clients.

In fact, if you work with me for coaching or done for you services, 9 times out of 10, Active Campaign will be part of your package.

Active Campaign allows you to get started for as little as $9 / month, and you can grow as your business does. That price doesn't include the CRM which is critical for most entrepreneurs, so count on a starting price of $49 / month which includes 1000 contacts, the CRM, and full automation.

But it's not just the low cost that has enamored me to ActiveCampaign. Once its setup, its much easier to operate the CRM than Infusionsoft, which is a big deal for busy sales reps. They also come out of the box with several gorgeous email templates that are fully mobile responsive. And creating new email templates is considerably easier than Infusionsoft and other options on the market.

Navigating the system is drop dead simple, the dashboard is easy to understand so you can see the current state of your marketing at a glance, and you can customize your own domain name within the URL's your customers see passing through the system.

ActiveCampaign doesn't come with as many features out of the box as Infusionsoft. It does have a form designer, but does not have landing pages, e-commerce, or as many reports. But in some ways that's an advantage. You can add those features as you want them, and instead of being locked into sub par built in solutions, you can purchase the best in breed options for whatever you want, and integrate them in.

ActiveCampaign integrates with hundreds of tools you'll need in your business quickly and easily. It's easy to tie together systems like WooCommerce, OptimizePress and other landing page and design tools, Zapier (which opens up hundreds of options), Membership systems, CRM's, and much more.

Advantages

- Get started very inexpensively and expand as your needs and business does.
- Easy to use and navigate.
- Intuitive Campaign / Automation Builder. We'll get to these in later chapters.
- Beautiful email templates right out of the box.
- Integrates with hundreds of tools for building e-commerce stores, landing pages, membership sites, online schools, and more.
- Custom domain branding.

Disadvantages

- No e-commerce components out of the box.
- No landing pages out of the box.
- Form designer has limited design options. Out of the box, the form designs look much better than Infusionsoft, but Infusionsoft allows more customization to make them look better with a little bit of work. Active Campaign is limited in options.
- Very few marketing reports.
- Smaller network of consultants, but more coming online all the time.
- Price goes up with more subscribers. So does Infusionsoft and most other options, but with Active Campaign the number of users between price jumps is lower.

I've worked with Infusionsoft a lot longer than Active Campaign, but in the short time I've been working with them, I've fallen in love with their platform and recommend it to most of my clients. There are a few "nice to haves" I'd like to see, but

ActiveCampaign is rapidly improving, and listening to their users. Infusionsoft on the other hand seems to have reached that plateau software companies often hit when they start to get too large (or get major investors like Goldman Sac's pulling the strings.)

I see great things for Active Campaign over the next few years.

Other Options

There are of course other automation systems on the market, but most come with a very large price tag. ActOn software, SmartSpring, and Marketo are 3 I have investigated and are incredibly powerful. But they have price tags to match.

Action Steps

Action step 1: Today's action step is easy, go to http://glenkowalski.com/activecampaign and get a 14-day trial of ActiveCampaign. In the next chapter you'll start using it.

If you prefer to use Infusionsoft, you can get it at http://glenkowalski.com/infusionsoft. Or if you already have a suite you are using, you should be able to tweak the steps outlined in the following chapter to match your software.

CHAPTER 8

Sales Pipeline

Part of attracting your clients is knowing how they're going to proceed down the sales path. So the next step we'll take is defining your sales pipeline. Whether you know it or not, you probably have some type of sales pipeline, but you might never have though about it or defined it before. We are going to define, systemize, and then automate it for you right now.

This chapter alone, if implemented, will make a monumental shift in your business practices and success.

Sales Pipeline or Marketing Funnel?

In the online marketing space, a sales pipeline is better known as a marketing funnel. Most of these are automatic and include selling products, and then automatically trying to up sell, down sell or cross sell related products.

For service providers or any business that involves one to one sales, I think calling it a sales pipeline is more appropriate and for many doesn't have the negative connotations of a sales funnel. With one on one sales, the image of a marketing funnel might imply you don't have any control over the process.

In a funnel, I envision leads falling through, with less and less leads making it to the bottom of the funnel and resulting in a sale. But that imagery hints gravity is in control of the flow whereas you aren't.

Besides, in a funnel, all the water eventually pours out the bottom (unless it leaks, which is another conversation). But that's not an accurate analogy because not all of your leads will become customers.

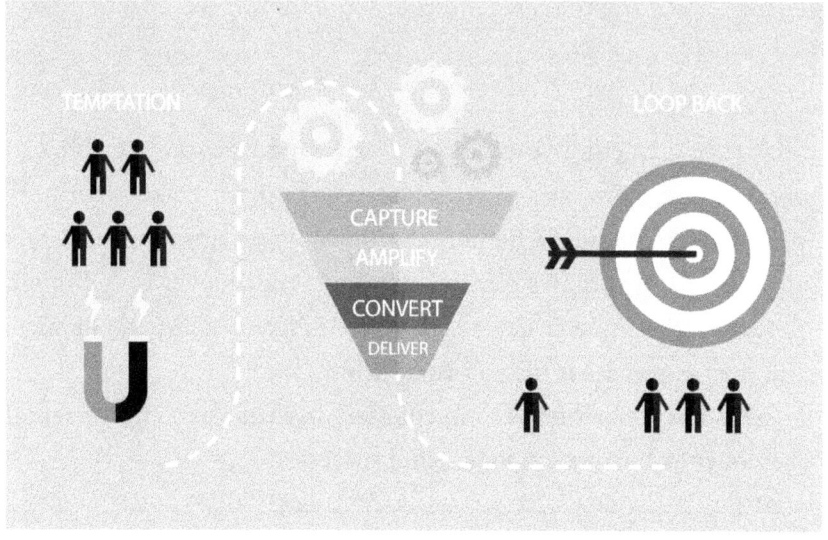

In a sales pipeline, you're moving your prospects throughout the buying cycle. I think it makes a more realistic visual, and it implies you have more control over the system. It also doesn't lead you down the path of spending too much time at the top of the funnel and allows you to strategically decide where to spend your time.

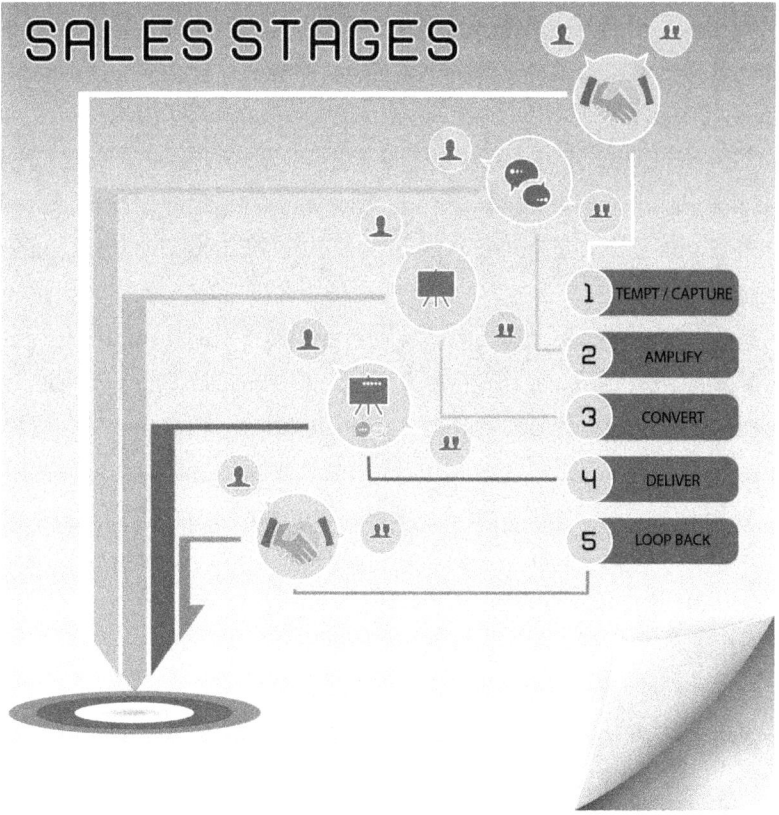

Personally I like this image a lot better, and it better illustrates how you are implementing the Unconventional Entrepreneur Automatic Marketing System.

Whatever you call it though, and it really doesn't matter, it's vital you realize how you treat your prospects, leads, and customers differently depending on where they are in your funnel, pipeline or probably most accurately sales process. And it's even more critical you spend the majority of your time in the right places.

With a marketing funnel, what often ends up happening for most business owners is lots of time is spent at the top of the funnel. Logically, this makes sense, as it is the widest part.

The problem is, the top of the funnel is also where you have the least amount of income, and can make the least impact for your clients. You require a huge volume of leads to make any impact.

It's the premium products at the end of your funnel you got into business to serve. But yet you spend the most time creating low impact / low income offers for businesses who aren't ready to commit.

What type of shift would you see in your business, if most of your time was spent in the premium areas of your business? These are the places where 85% of more of your income is created. So why not spend more time there. A pipeline metaphor might make it easier for you to focus on the income generation activities a funnel doesn't.

Why You Need a Pipeline (or Funnel)

Think of your pipeline as the path your clients will take in their interactions with you. If the Unconventional Entrepreneur Automatic Marketing System is the set of processes and strategies, think of your pipeline as a road map.

With a roadmap in place, you never have to wonder what to do next. Your sales reps never have to question how to proceed. And even the people who fulfill your services and / or take the money know exactly what their next steps are going to be.

The beauty of always knowing what's happening next is it allows you the opportunity to automate those next steps. Whether it be firing off an automatic email thanking your prospect for attending a discovery session, or sending an automated up sell for a higher level coaching program after enrollment, much of your increased revenue and free time plan can be implemented on autopilot because this roadmap guides your process towards your maximum revenues and your free time.

Imagine the extra reserves in your tank by not having to think about next steps, and in fact having them happen for you automatically. I told you earlier this chapter is transformational.

What is Your Pipeline?

Let's discuss your pipeline for a moment. We don't want to spend a lot of time there because it can and will be adjusted over time. Facebook has posters up all over their walls that say, "Done is better than perfect." This is one of those cases where we're going to adopt that same mindset because as you progress through, implement, work in, and analyze your success system; you'll always be improving this process over time.

Whether you know it or not, you already have a pipeline. It might change over time, but if you've been working in your business for any length of time you'll notice patterns and regularities you work on.

For example, someone may call your office and setup an appointment to talk to you. You'll have an initial conversation, or maybe a discovery session. Then you'll do some type of follow-up and eventually try to make an offer and collect the money.

Eventually (hopefully), you'll try to sell your clients other products or move them towards bigger things.

And then you'll go on to fulfill your services.

Why this is so Powerful

Here is why having a pipeline, as part of your automation system, is so powerful. Let's say a new lead enters your system. Maybe they download a report from your website.

You could immediately trigger off an email, or a series of emails prompting the new lead to book a discovery session with you. This would all happen on autopilot without any intervention on your part at all.

When the user books a discovery session, they will move to the next stage in the pipeline. This move could then trigger off an initial mail confirming the meeting has been set. It could send a reminder a day before and / or an hour before the session so your new prospect doesn't forget and need to reschedule. This saves you time due to wasted missed meetings.

The system would also send you an email letting you know about the meeting, and create a task / appointment in your calendar. You'll see at a glance everything you know about the prospect and their behavior so you are ready to prepare.

After the meeting, all you need to do is move your prospects status to Discovery session complete. Your system can then send you and / or your prospect a mail with next steps, set tasks and appointments, different follow up, forms to fill in, invoices, or whatever you need.

And so on through the pipeline or roadmap.

Do you see the power having this roadmap in place gives your business? I'm sure you're already seeing how much time will be saved out of your day just from having this in place.

Your pipeline can be as simple or as complex as you need. But at a minimum, I recommend it includes at least 4 stages.

- A stage where a new lead needs to be contacted.
- A stage where you are in contact, and talking to the lead.
- And a Won or
- Lost stage.

Action Steps

Action Step 1: Write out what your current process is step by step in the format of the example below.

If you don't have a current process, or if you're just starting out, this is going to be transformational for you. You can start with our example pipeline, which has been proven across multiple businesses and multiple industries. It is modeled after a business that needs to provide quotes or estimates, so as a service provider you might be able to get away with less steps, like in example 2 below.

Example 1.
1. New Opportunity or New Lead that Needs Follow up
2. Initial Meeting Booked.
3. Initial Meeting Completed.
4. Quote / Proposal Sent to Client.
5. Quote Approved.
6. Invoice Sent to Client
7. Won / Signed
8. Lost / Not Signed

Example 2.
1. To Contact
2. Discovery Session Booked
3. Discovery Session Complete

4. Signed Contract and Payment (Won)
5. No Contract (Lost)

Obviously both of these example pipelines could be shorter or longer. They can also lead into other pipelines. For example, you could have an initial pipeline for brand new clients, but then a much shorter one to sell a different service to existing clients.

I recommend at a minimum you start with either example 1 or example 2 depending on whether your business uses a quote based system or collects the initial check at the discovery session.

Action Step 2: Sign into ActiveCampaign and go to Deals. If you're using Infusionsoft or another system, you process will vary slightly.

After going to Deals, look at the default pipeline. You can add new stages on the right, and move around the stages with drag and drop. ActiveCampaign supports multiple pipelines, so you can create as many different pipelines as you need, or play around with some draft versions.

Here's an example of how your pipeline may look if you are using ActiveCampaign. This one has 5 stages···

- New contacts to be contacted
- Contacts you're talking to
- Contact you've booked (but not had) a discovery session with
- Contacts you've met with, but who haven't closed.

After that, the contacts are either won or lost which isn't shown in the pipeline.

ActiveCampaign Deals Screen

If you're using Infusionsoft, you setup the sales pipeline in your *CRM --> Settings --> Sales Pipeline.* You'll notice there's no drag and drop interface, but instead an order value. I recommend you leave big gaps (i.e. 10, 20, 30) between pipeline stages, because in the future if you want to add a new stage you'll be able to do so without reordering every step.

Here's a complex pipeline with 13 stages. Notice the order is only 1 – 10 before taking a jump. If you wanted to insert a new stage, you'd have to renumber all of the stages. That's why I recommend the numbers in the Order column be intervals of 10. Also notice with Infusionsoft, you can add target days and probability for each stage, which is great for forecasting. You can also add a checklist for each stage.

Sales Pipeline

Stage						**Rebuild Pipeline**
Name						
Order	0					
Target # Days	0					
Probability	0					

Edit	Name	Target # days	Probability	Order	Checklist	Delete
Edit...	New Opportunity (From Web)	1	5	0	Checklist...	Delete
Edit...	Potential Lead	1	5	1	Checklist...	Delete
Edit...	Attempted Contact	28	3	2	Checklist...	Delete
Edit...	In Progress	7	5	3	Checklist...	Delete
Edit...	Qualified	10	8	4	Checklist...	Delete
Edit...	Contract Sent	5	9	5	Checklist...	Delete
Edit...	Contract Signed	0	10	6	Checklist...	Delete
Edit...	Order Confirmation / Inv Sent	5	15	7	Checklist...	Delete
Edit...	Funding	1	75	8	Checklist...	Delete
Edit...	Funds Received	0	85	9	Checklist...	Delete
Edit...	Final Statement Sent to Sales	3	99	10	Checklist...	Delete
Edit...	Lost	0	0	18	Checklist...	Delete
Edit...	Won	0	100	18	Checklist...	Delete

Infusionsoft Sales Pipeline Screen

This action item should only take you about 10 minutes to setup so you won't spend a lot of time here now. As you work through the Unconventional Entrepreneur Automatic Marketing System book you'll see in more detail how all the stages of the pipeline fit together and how you'll use and automate each stage. It's likely working through the system will cause you to make changes in the pipeline to suit how you want to work going forward.

For now, you want the basic steps setup so you can see how the system works, and your customer roadmap is setup before digging into the nitty gritty. Baby steps now will save you overlapping learning the software and learning the success system all at the same time. You'll also notice many new opportunities for further automation and time saving, revenue boosting tweaks as you implement and work with the system.

Like everything else in marketing your system and pipeline will evolve over time and testing. But by having the system and framework in place now, making those adjustments are both efficient and measurable, ensuring you are truly moving closer to your goals with every iteration.

Go create your pipeline now, and then let's move onto attracting boatloads of your ideal customers and clients.

CHAPTER 9

Attract More Clients with the Temptation Mechanism

Now that you know what you're selling, are clear on who you are selling to, and have your initial pipeline setup, it's time to start attracting your ideal clients and showing them what you offer. As you work through this chapter, you'll understand why the targeting part of our system in earlier chapters was so important.

Trying to attract interest without that picture in your mind can be a frustrating and expensive experience.

This chapter focuses on online marketing and attraction since that's the point of this book. Since I am based in Panama, and work internationally, online marketing is the most efficient, and often only, marketing avenue open to me. But the rules, recommendations, and strategies spelled out here will apply across lead generation methodology.

Attraction involves spending time around your ideal clients. And while part of this time will be spent online, there are plenty of offline venues as well. And you should be exploiting every available means necessary. This includes networking and direct outreach. In fact, networking and direct outreach, especially in the early stages of your business, tend to bring faster results than online avenues which take some time to build. This book doesn't dive too deep into those avenues because there are many books, courses, and seminars available. And most of the attraction principles in this chapter can be utilized offline anyway.

The beauty of a customer relationship manager (CRM) setup as part of your automated marketing is once your leads are in the system, they will be automatically marketed to and followed up with as per the way they entered your sales pipeline. It doesn't matter whether they entered your system through online or offline methods, once they are in the system, the system takes over.

Website / Platform

The core component of your online marketing is your website. It's where your clients learn more about you, sign up for your services, and is the central place in your platform.

It's also critical to your attraction efforts and everything you do in your business. However, I want to be very clear... Your website is NOT your lead generation system, and I almost never recommend paying money to send traffic to it directly. Certainly not to your home page.

I want to get that statement out of the way in case you read this section and go out an buy a bunch of paid traffic without setting up your system the way I recommend.

More importantly, if you are currently spending money on traffic, and sending that traffic to your home page, stop now. Turn off the traffic spigot before you waste another cent. I guess there are very few cases where you want to send paid traffic to your home page... Like because you have a bunch of extra advertising budget lying around, and you want to spend it without generating new leads.

There are a few exceptions we'll talk about, like if your home page is your lead generation page, and follows certain rules. But if you have a normal website, with a home page and multiple sub pages, you almost never want to send traffic to it directly.

Ok, now that's out of the way, what is the point of a website?

Like I said earlier, the website is the core of your platform, and in today's day and age, you're expected to have one. If nothing else, you need it to prove you're a professional, and that you run a real business. If you tell me you're a business owner, but you don't have a website, my first thought is you don't take your business very seriously, and wonder why would I trust you with my hard earned dollars? Everyone might not be a hard ass like me, but how many "real" businesses do you know that don't have a website?

The next reason is, it is a vital part of your attraction system. Your ideal clients will only buy from you if they know, like, and trust you. And a big part of that is the ability to go to your website and read more about you, your company, and your processes or what you can offer.

It should showcase your knowledge, and more importantly demonstrate what you can do for your clients. And why you're absolutely the best choice for whatever driving need they have, that you solve. It becomes your soapbox for everything you do, both online and off, which is why we call it a platform.

As an aside, I've had several conversations with "business owners" and service providers who think a website is no longer required thanks to Facebook, LinkedIn and other social media outlets that allow company pages. In fact, I know a number of business owners who do exactly that. And they're doing fine.

But what happens when Facebook is no longer the powerhouse it is today? Don't think that'll ever happen? Why not go ask anyone who staked their claim on MySpace. Or what if they change their policies to make it more difficult to do business? Did you know thanks to a recent change in Facebook policy only about 10% of your business followers see any given post to your business page newsfeed? 100% of your blog subscribers however will see and be emailed posts you put on your own website.

The same is true for "free" website platforms like Wordpress.org, Blogger, and Wax. I hear a lot of advice from consultants telling you it's fine to start with these free platforms and then move up later but I disagree if you are serious about your business.

What happens if one of these platforms shuts down? You are out of business instantly.

Even if they don't shut down, at some point you'll want to project a professional image and have your own domain instead of piggy backing off someone else's business. At that point you have the huge cost of trying to migrate, updating marketing materials, and rebuilding your brand. I've done it often. Trust me, it sucks and you don't want that hassle.

Free platforms are fine for a hobby, but if you have a real business, spend the 15 bucks to get your own domain name, and 10 - 25 bucks a month for hosting.

I understand some people are bootstrapped, and need to build their businesses up from zero. But if you're in that stage, you're probably not ready for this system yet, you just need to hustle, probably in person, and make a few bucks first.

I admire what you're trying to do, I really do. So if you are really in that state of need, and you are 100% committed to building a business, but you honestly can't afford 15 bucks (or less) for your own domain, return this book to me, and I will purchase 1 year of domain registration for you, with an available domain name of your choice.

At any point in the future, if you've built your business up to the point where you're not struggling, and want to take it to the next level, give me a call and I'll send you an up to date copy of your book absolutely free. It's my small way of being able to help, I've been there, and while the Unconventional Entrepreneur Automatic Marketing System will help you grow your business at hyper drive, there are other things that take priority and you need first.

Creating Your Platform and Website

Before we begin, this book isn't about website design or platform building, I should have a book about those out soon. Both of those topics deserve books of their own, and I plan to put out a platform book in the future. But this chapter will give you an introduction to the basics you need to get started.

Fortunately, creating your website doesn't have to be expensive or difficult. Get a hosting plan, install Wordpress, pick a theme, and you are off to the races.

Once again, there are many books on website design, and also plenty of designers who can make sure your page is professional and becomes a vital part of your attraction system. But there are a couple of things many business owners (and website designers) miss when creating a site that are critical. So we'll cover those here.

Professionalism

Your website should convey an image appropriate to the brand you want to project and your ideal clients. It will vary depending on who you are talking to. Obviously, the website for a lawyer will look different from one for a love coach. Certain professional services will have a very strict academic look, while others can be more fun. But regardless of who you are speaking to, you don't want to come across in a way that repels you from your ideal client.

Your site should be easy to navigate, not some confusing mess that looks great but where your client has no idea with what to do next. Their next steps should be immediately obvious at all times.

Mobile Ready / Responsive

Every year more and more online readers - your clients - spend more time on their phones browsing the internet. And less time on their desktops. This is especially true if you do any advertising on Facebook and other Social Media where over 50% of all views will be from a mobile device. If your site looks terrible on a small screen, your ideal clients will immediately click away, never to return.

Conveys Your USP Immediately

Remember in the action step of chapter 3, you crafted a Unique Selling Proposition for your company. That USP needs to leap off the home page (and every page) of your website. You can't attract clients if no one know what you do, or what makes you different.

I can't tell you the number of sites I visit every day and I have no idea of what they do, who they do it for, or how they get it done. When that happens, attraction is dead, and anyone viewing your site will move on.

One great way to do convey this message is with a small explainer video that let's browsers know your USP in 30 seconds to 1 minute.

But it is also done through your headlines, sub points, bullets and body text.

Contains a Blog or Video Blog

Ok, this one is somewhat optional for certain businesses, however its optional for fewer businesses every year. Your content makes up the core of your attraction system. If you plan on receiving any organic traffic from the search engines, you'll almost certainly need a blog. Also, without a blog, you don't have a platform to communicate from, it's your first touch point with many of your ideal clients.

It's how they get to know, like and trust you.

Has the Ability to Accept Plugins and Integrate With Your Automation System

This is the most important technical requirement for implementing the *Unconventional Entrepreneur Automatic Marketing System*. You won't be able to automate your marketing if your web platform doesn't allow this step. Or at best it will cost you substantial custom development costs to get it all integrated.

Most common web development platforms have the ability to integrate with your automation system. Even if you have a raw HTML site, programmed from scratch (very expensive, and not very user friendly or scalable), you can usually have your web developer add a little piece of code.

This plugin, module, or code snippet gets added to every page of your site, and allows your automation system to monitor traffic and user activity so you can automate your marketing based on real prospect activities. The power in this can't be underestimated.

You'll also need the ability to integrate forms for later steps in the system so you can collect leads, setup access connected to your automation system, run shopping carts, and more.

In Wordpress, the platform I strongly recommend for 99 out of 100 entrepreneurs, its called a plugin, and you can get to it from your dashboard. It's and easy step if you do any backend web work at all. Or easily done by your consultant / technical help if not.

Action Steps

Action Step 1: Go to your automation tool, and find the plugin, download it, and install it on your site.

In ActiveCampaign, the code to track user activity is easy to find and use. Log into the system, go to apps, make sure Site Events is enabled, click on it, and you'll see a code block. Add that code to every page on your site and you're site is now ready to be monitored.

On the left hand side, make sure you add any domains you'll be running that code on are listed or it will be ignored.

You can also add code for different events on your website from here. This is a little more of an advanced concept, but in a nutshell if there's any type of behavior you'd like to monitor, you can do so with the code in this section.

In Infusionsoft, there's a plugin you can download. Other systems will have other means, but their documentation should explain the steps to get this integrated.

Identify Keywords or Problem Language Your Ideal Clients Use

Regardless of whether you plan on getting organic search traffic (traffic coming from search engines like Google), paid advertising, forums / social media, or direct outreach, you need to understand the language your ideal clients use when describing their problems or looking for the service you provide.

Notice I said describing their problems, not looking for your service. Many of your ideal clients, in fact I'd venture to say most of them, don't know they're looking for you. All they know, is they have a problem and they want to find the fix.

They're online looking for the solution. They go to seminars or trade shows looking for the solution. They even hope to find the solution at networking events they attend.

In the search and advertising world, this language is known as keywords or key phrases. The traditional meaning of those words have lost some of their value as Google implements better artificial intelligence into what people are asking for, but you still need to understand how your ideal clients talk and describe they're wants and needs.

What are their problems? Big problems and more specific problems?

I want a better asset protection plan. (Big problem)

I need to protect my gold coins in case my cheating wife goes after them in the divorce. (Specific problem)

Obviously in your business there's a wide range between big problems and small problems. I'd describe a big problem as a problem that takes multiple steps and a long time to fix.

A small problem can usually be fixed in a matter of minutes often with just one step.

So using our example above, I want a better behaved dog will take a 6 week training program, meeting 2 times a week, with a follow up session at 3 months and 1 year.

If on the other hand, I need my dog to stop peeing on my favorite plant, it might just require spraying your miracle pet repellent spray on your favorite plant one time and the problem is solved.

One of the fastest ways to identify keywords, is to use Google's Ad Words tool. Google's advertising mechanism is based on keywords, so the tool will help identify profitable keywords for future advertising and for exposing keywords for SEO purposes. I also find it useful to look up problem language.

Just start with a question you think your ideal customer is asking, and it will recommend variants. Once you have a number of possibilities, you can click to see example websites using those. You'll also find examples of program language just by typing in your suspected questions into the search bar.

Blogs especially are great for seeking out and identifying problem language. Especially once you start reading through the comments. Start looking for blogs within your niche. Scroll down to the comment section and read through the comments to discover problem language your clients are using.

Identifying problem language and keywords is similar to other market research in that it's not difficult, but can take a lot of time and work.

Identify Where Your Ideal Clients Are Hanging Out

As you're investigating your keywords and problem language you're going to notice patterns about where your ideal clients are spending time. The search exercise you did above is especially helpful in this area. This will range from blogs, where you'll see their engagement in the comments, to forums, to social media like Facebook.

The key to attracting your ideal client is spending time in the places where they're hanging out and gradually putting yourself out there. That doesn't mean sending a bunch of spam, or cramming your service into their faces. But join in on the conversations, inject help wherever you can, and be a good citizen.

Eventually your prospects will start noticing you.

Finding out where your ideal customers are also helps you identify where to best spend advertising dollars. You don't want to spend hundreds of dollars per month advertising on some social media platform none of your clients are hanging out on or engaged with.

While we're discussing it though, for most businesses, Facebook is an ideal starting place. Regardless of what your demographic is, chances are very good a significant portion of your ideal clients is using Facebook. And Facebook's targeting options allow you to narrow down exactly on the person you identified in chapter 3. Because I work with Unconventional Entrepreneurs, a lot of my client's ideal clients are very aware of privacy issues. But even they seem to be on Facebook.

Action Steps

Action Step 1: Identify 5 - 10 keywords your ideal client uses when looking for their problem, or your solution.

Action Step 2: Download the problem language and worksheet from http://glenkowalski.com/problemlanguage.

Action Step 3: List 50 - 100 examples of problem language your ideal clients are using. This can be extremely eye opening for how you word your ads, and even your offer itself.

Action Step 4: List out 3 to 5 places (social platforms, forums, blogs, networking events, etc.) where your ideal client is hanging out.

Action Step 5: If using Infusionsoft or an Automation System that uses Lead Source, setup a Lead Source for each one.

Action Step 6: Go to Facebook Business and create a new Facebook Ad Account. Creating the account only takes a few minutes, doesn't cost anything, and there's lots of help available. We'll discuss what to do with your ad account in the next chapter.

Automation in the Attraction Process

Marketing automation makes identifying problem language and determining where your clients are spending time easier and more effective because once setup, it records the source of all your traffic. That way, as you move forward with your business, and gather more data, you'll be able to better focus advertising and marketing efforts. And you'll know exactly how well your efforts are performing.

Throughout the Unconventional Entrepreneur Automatic Marketing System, recording and analyzing data is critical because it is the key step that allows you to gain the most efficiency, and in the shortest amount of time.

Gaining Credibility

While we're talking about your temptation system, nothing is more tempting than credibility. Credibility can be grown in a number of ways ranging from books to social proof, and public speaking to webinars. But the most important part is getting your name in front of those ideal clients, and being visible everywhere.

That's easier to do now that you know where your users are hanging out. And listening to their problem language while providing solutions.

That brings us to the culmination of everything you've learned about attraction in your business and building the automatic attraction system.

Seducing Your Ideal Clients

Your first step to seducing your ideal clients is identifying and tempting them with one small problem or issue they're having, right now, today. Now do you understand why the above research is so important?

Ideally, this is something you can solve, or at least explain, within 5 - 15 minutes. You want this solution to be as focused as possible, but to hit on a burning desire.

One of the best examples of this I saw in the dating niche, where the solution they were offering was "How to know if your date is ready to be kissed."

It spoke to a desperate need - how to know the girl you are out on a date with is ready for you to kiss her. And offered up a solution that took about 2 minutes to read and implement. Yes, I bought it. Hook , line, and sinker.

Imagine putting an easy to implement solution in front of the ideal client, right in the place where they are hanging out. Do you think it'd be possible for that client to not be tempted enough to give you their email address? Do you think you'll have established a ton of credibility in your industry?

Having that solution will have that client seeking out more information about who you are, and what you do. And in the next chapter, we'll discuss how to actually take that interest, and turn it into leads for your business starting as soon as tomorrow.

Action Steps

Action Step 1: Based on the problem language / keyword exercise you did above, brainstorm as many ideas as you can for fast easy problems your ideal clients are running into, and you can solve in a matter of minutes.

CHAPTER 10

Capture Leads

Getting people interested in your services, by hanging out where they spend time, is a great step towards building your business. But everyone knows most people who visit your webpage don't stick around long. And once they leave, they're gone for good. They could have every intention of coming back, but they won't.

Life gets in the way, or they delete their cache and don't remember your website, or they get tempted by the next shiny object, or they plain flake. Whatever the cause, you have a limited amount of time to make a first impression, so your first priority needs to be capturing enough information to stay in front of them.

Capturing leads during the temptation phase of your attraction process is critical. If you do nothing else for your online business, this step alone will at least give you a list of people you can approach. It's the rest of the system that turns leads to revenue. But if you don't capture leads first, the rest of the system is useless, and a waste of precious time.

In an earlier chapter, you learned your website doesn't capture leads. And you almost never send traffic to your home page.

Instead, you send traffic to landing pages, lead generation pages, or as I like to call them, temptation pages.

These pages are part of your website, but separate, and they only have one goal, to capture the email, name, and possibly other information from the person visiting the site. And if possible, on their first visit. And if not possible, to set a Facebook or retargeting pixel which allows you to continue marketing to them via other platforms. We'll discuss pixels more in chapters 12 and 13.

They do that by entering the conversation your client is already having in your mind.

The Landing / Temptation Page

As we stated earlier, the landing page is a special page on your site. Ideally, it has no navigation on it, other than mandatory legal terms of service, and a large call to action. The action you want your prospects to take, is giving you some information like an email address, phone number, or other information.

Sounds simple enough, but here's the rub. No one's willing hand over his or her personal information to a stranger. So you must offer something tempting in return. If the creature from the black lagoon asks my phone number, I'm running the other direction. Jessica Alba does it, I'm tempted, even though I'm very happily married.

This is known as a lead magnet or a bribe. You have to "sell" that lead magnet or bribe well enough the potential client knows it's worth giving up that information. Every year, as more and more businesses capture leads this way, this gets more difficult.

In the last chapter, you came up with a list of problems your ideal clients NEED to be solved and that you solve.

This is the first place you'll use that list.

Pick your hottest item from the list. What problem are your clients facing right now? What is their burning desire?

Ideally, the problem is narrowly focused. I.e. How to grow a big business is too wide for a lead magnet. However, 3 steps to increasing your lead flow this week in 5 minutes or less would be much more targeted. And it's even better if it's a problem you can solve in 15 minutes or less.

"The magic word you can put in your next email that will double your sales tomorrow," would be ideal.

Next name the solution and decide how you will package it up into a useful format for potential clients. There are several ways to accomplish this, and your goal is deciding the most powerful and useful format, and then producing it for your audience.

Lead Magnet Ideas

E-Books, White Papers, and Reports

These are the oldest forms of lead magnets available. They even predate the web. They've been around so long, for one reason, because they work. E-Books are a little long to consume quickly and / or to solve one problem, so they don't always make the best bribe, but they are an option.

Reports and white papers convert better than e-books in most cases.

Physical Books

Physical books, because they are physical and have a high-perceived value, can be excellent.

You present yourself as a published author, and your ideal prospects will jump at the chance to learn more about you. There's a technique to doing this, but it can be incredibly powerful.

I recently spoke at a book fair about a book I haven't even published yet, and the response was amazing. Almost everyone at the presentation lined up to put in his or her name.

Webinars and Webcasts

Webinars and other webcasts are growing into the most common lead generation tools available today. But I prefer them as part of the education or amplification phase you'll learn in the next chapter. For attracting leads they don't convert as well as other delivery mechanisms because they need too high of a commitment from new prospects.

Later in the book, you'll discover a complete formula for creating a lead generation and sales funnels using webcasts and webinars strategically to shorten the time frame from cold to a sale.

Videos

People love video, and more video is consumed every day. Instructional videos your ideal clients can watch right away that answer their burning questions or solve their problems make great lead magnets.

However, I've found that videos make a better "middle of the funnel" offer than top of the funnel. Reports have a higher perceived value as a lead magnet, and video landing pages at the top of the funnel don't convert as good as straight short text.

I know many marketers who use these successfully at the top of the funnel as an attraction tool, but my testing shows they work better later.

Checklists and Lists

Is there a checklist your ideal client can use that will make their life or work easier? Or are they missing an important step towards their goals? These make great bribes because they are easy to consume, and because you can make new ones or change them in a heartbeat.

Blind Sales Ads

Most often done with video, these are information pieces that solve the client's immediate issues, but then lead them directly to a sale of another item. These can be risky but powerful. Make sure you present value and solve the immediate wish, or you will break your prospects trust.

This technique works awesome for leading into webinars, and the Unconventional Entrepreneur Attraction Process webinar breaks down exactly how to do this.

Note, like in the paragraph I wrote about videos above, these work better when joined with a report or book as the lead magnet itself, and then these ads presented inside the thank you page.

Info graphics, Courses, and Other Information

Virtually any delivery mechanism you can think of, as long as it answers the question or problem you promised on your landing page, can deliver your lead magnet. Try several, test which one works best, and then send the majority of your traffic to it.

There's nothing wrong with having different lead magnets since everyone is unique and looking for something different. If one bribe doesn't resonate with them, another one might. The companies with the most (targeted) lead magnets get the most leads.

The Nuts and Bolts of your Temptation Page

Temptation / landing page design and copy, like sales page design and copy, is part art, part science, and according to some, part magic. Fortunately automation helps you to test and track various aspects of your temptation page until you get exactly what you want.

This book can't get into all the mechanics needed build the perfect landing page, since that could take several books on its own, but some components absolutely have to be there. And I'll give you some resources to help.

Headline

Your headline should make a big bold promise of what you will deliver with your lead magnet. As long as you deliver what you promise, bigger is better.

There's an old sales myth telling you that you should under promise and over deliver.

I say bull crap. Grant Cordone nailed it when he said, "Over promise AND over deliver."

Many marketers do the first. Your job is to nail the second.

Sub-Headline

This is the place for you to expand on your promise. Give short details, facts, numbers, etc. You can also deliver on the "how" of your promise.

Body Copy

According to most recent tests, body copy for a lead magnet should be kept short. But this needs testing for your industry. A normal rule of thumb is the more money or commitment you are asking for up front, the longer your copy needs to be.

The important thing here is to let the prospect know the benefits they'll get from consuming your magnet.

Your body should expand on your hook you created in an earlier chapter.

A Picture of Your Bribe

Most testing of landing pages done across industries proves that having an image of your bribe - like the picture of an e-book, will help it convert at a higher rate. There are many exceptions to this rule. For example, Motley Fool uses plain boring text based ads, and you know they are testing every aspect of their pages. For them, for at least certain offers, the plain ads do better.

Different styles of images should be tested. Photographs of real people also work great, especially if they're looking directly at the camera or CTA.

Lead Capture Form (or CTA that pops up your capture form)

And finally, the leads capture form. This is the main integration between your automation system and your website.

And the most important part of the temptation page. This is the form that your leads fill out to get access to whatever piece of value you're offering.

The amount of information you gather on your form will depend on a variety of factors, and will also need to be tested.

At the least, you'll need an email address, and preferably a first name. With that data, you can send follow-up information. Later, you can guide your prospect to another online form where you'll capture more information. Or you can ask them to email you with a phone number, etc.

You Can Ask For Anything

However, these forms can also ask for anything else you need before working with a client. This includes phone numbers, income, net worth, birthdates, career, or anything else you feel is important.

But, you need to keep in mind the more information you ask, the more friction leads will experience. In other words, the more difficult you make it, and the more information you ask for, the less leads you'll get.

You need to find a balancing point between lead count and lead quality. Leads who give you more information are more qualified leads.

Once again, testing is vital. On some forms, just adding a phone number can reduce the response rate by 50% or more. Decide whether it's worth losing half your leads to get that information.

One way to mitigate massive friction, and increase quantity of leads, while only spending time with the most qualified, is building a funnel. Start with a lead magnet that asks for only first name and email. Then give your client more information about how you can solve their problems and get them the desired results. Lead them towards another landing page that offers a bigger bribe, but also requires more information.

A typical example is a webinar (either free or paid) or free consultation. In the industry, these types of offers are often called a tripwire or welcome mat, thanks to Ryan Deiss, Perry Belcher and Frank Kern. We discuss those more in chapters 8, 9, and 10.

Landing Page Software

Landing page design is part art and part design. In the past, business owners like yourself needed to hire a team of designers, programmers, and copy experts just to get your landing page up and running. And every time you wanted to make a slight change, you needed to call them up, pay hundreds of dollars per hour, and wait a week to get your changes.

Today, there exist several beautiful landing page options on the market that get you 50% of the way to the landing page of your dreams. The remaining 50% is marketing copy (or the words you use), so there's no need to hire programmers unless you need complex custom integrations.

OptimizePress, Lead Pages, Unbounce, and Click Funnels are 4 big players in the landing page builder market. All of them have several gorgeous templates and are easy to customize via drag and drop interfaces. Each package has advantages and disadvantages so investigate them thoroughly. There's no easy path to migrate between them if you start with one and then use a different one. So any pages you want you'd need to start from scratch.

You can intermix most of the tools if you have to, so if you have one lead magnet on one system, you could, in theory, create a new lead magnet and put it on a different system. This could be a maintenance nightmare though, so make your best effort in choosing the correct platform off the bat.

Fortunately, each of the options I've listed above come with trial versions and / or money-back guarantees so you can play with them before choosing.

Automating Your Lead Capture

Once you've decided on the fields your form should have, you'll build your form in your Automation System. You'll eventually move that form to your landing page, but not yet. Build it in your automation system first.

This process varies depending on the system you use. In ActiveCampaign, you'll start by creating a list. This list will contain all the contacts you want segmented by the lead magnet they consumed.

Further segmentation is possible within ActiveCampaign as you can segment by demographics, behavior and other factors. This is a more advanced concept you'll add later.

Infusionsoft on the other hand, doesn't use lists, instead it has one big list that can be segmented by tags. Other systems will have different approaches, but their help system should point you in the right direction.

After the list is created, you'll create the lead capture form.

In Infusionsoft, you'll do this as part of a campaign, so you'll go to your Campaign builder and create a new campaign. The Infusionsoft marketplace has a ton of free campaigns you can use as a starting point, or you can build one from scratch. Either way, one of the earliest stages in the campaign will be your form.

Within the campaign builder there's a form designer you can use to customize your form in any way you can imagine.

ActiveCampaign is simpler in you have to click on the "create a new form" option and attach it to the list you created earlier.

You'll then be taken to the form area where you can make limited customizations to your form.

Both Infusionsoft and ActiveCampaign are limited in custom design options for your forms. Infusionsoft has better control over individual colors and field sizes. ActiveCampaign, only has a few different options.

ActiveCampaign forms though, in my opinion, look better out of the box.

Besides, thanks to the magic of integration, many landing page and form designers have add-ons you can use for your landing page to make your form appear the way you envision. So you can actually work with best in breed software to get the design you want while leaving the magic of marketing automation to your automation system. I am a big fan of using best in breed solutions for every part of the Unconventional Entrepreneur Automatic Marketing System.

Most of the landing page solutions I mentioned earlier have elaborate forms that will integrate directly with the form you created. So the prospects see your awesome visual form while the automation form code does the work under the covers.

In either app, once you have your form set up, anyone who fills out the form will be automatically added to your Customer Relationship Management (CRM) system and you'll be able to add many types of automation. For example you can set triggers to notify your sales team, send follow up mails, add tags or little pieces of information, schedule follow-up calls, and almost anything else you can imagine. If you want someone on your sales team to follow up, you'll also add the contact to a sales pipeline.

Your sales team will follow up in minutes instead of hours or days. Statistics show after 5 minutes, your response rate drops almost 95%. It drops off completely in a matter of days, so it's critical follow up happens as soon as possible.

Now you'll never worry about missing leads ever again.

We'll be adding much of this automation later in the system, but two pieces of automation need to be added now. That's the confirmation mail(s) and delivery mechanism.

Double Opt In Confirmation

Spam laws are getting tougher worldwide, and you never want to send mail to anyone who doesn't want to receive it. For that reason, double opt in has become the standard.

What this means is, after your prospect fills out the form, you'll send an automatic mail asking them to confirm their request. Once they confirm, they'll be marked and added to your list.

The downside of double opt in confirmation is that many people will miss the follow up mail. Like friction, this will reduce your lead count. But then again, leads that double opt in, are more likely to become customers, anyway.

Confirmation and Delivery

Whether you use double opt in or not, you must send a confirmation mail. This mail will let your prospect know you've received their request and have a link to their lead magnet thank you page. If delivery of the magnet cannot be automated (like a physical mailer for example), you'll let your prospect know when and how they'll be receiving it.

This mail is also used to welcome the prospect to your tribe, or group, and to set expectations. Its a good idea to let them know right away how often they'll hear from you, what information you'll be sending, and how they can unsubscribe if they no longer want to receive your mail.

It's a great idea to give them next steps such as liking your Facebook page, calling you, setting up spam filters, etc. Most businesses skip this, which gives you a powerful competitive advantage when you add one.

In Infusionsoft, you must add your double opt in step and all the follow up and conversion mails. In ActiveCampaign all of this is taken care of for you, you'll just have to customize the mail the way you want within the form design area itself. The double opt in will automatically run and send your confirmation mails at the proper times.

Integrating Your Form

Once you've created your form, your confirmation mails and lead magnet delivery system added, and everything from the automation side is set to run, you need to integrate your form on your site.

There are 2 ways this can happen.

1. Code Integration

Both ActiveCampaign and Infusionsoft will give you a little piece of code to add to your website in the place you want the form to appear. Other systems will do something similar. This could be a short JavaScript block or a much longer block of HTML and script code. Which one you use will depend on your individual situation.

If you are technically inclined, adding this piece of code to your page is a matter of copying it from your automation system, and pasting it in the right spot.

However, you also have the choice to email this code to your web designer. This is often an easier choice if you aren't a web programmer yourself.

Wordpress and other website platforms have a habit of messing with your code, so sometimes just pasting it in isn't enough and you have to build wrappers, or stick the form code inside of short codes. If either of those 2 terms or foreign to you, call your web guy to install the code for you.

2. Tool Integration

A much more polished choice that looks better 9 out of 10 times is to integrate your form with a form builder or your landing page software. Using this solution, you'll "hook up" your software to your automation account and tell it which form you want to use.

You can then make very nice graphical opt in boxes which match the look and feel of your site.

All the landing page solutions we discussed above integrate out of the box with either Infusionsoft or ActiveCampaign, or most other automation and Auto-responder applications. That's one reason I prefer ActiveCampaign to Infusionsoft. Sure Infusionsoft gives better customization options, but when you want your forms to look great, you're better off using a company that specializes in that.

Action Steps

Action Step 1: Investigate the various landing page software options listed above. Pick one that sounds best for your needs and get a trial account or buy it (they all have money-back guarantees).

Action Step 2: Pick which problem or question you want to solve and create a lead magnet that delivers on its promise.

Action Step 3: Write the copy and design a landing page that "sells" your lead magnet for an email address and name. Create any required thank you or confirmation pages.

Action Step 4: Create a New Form in your Automation software, Add the required confirmation steps and emails.

Action Step 5: Integrate your new form into your landing page. Test the entire process.

Action Step 6: Promote your landing pages.

Yes, you are finally capturing leads. Feels great, doesn't it?

Action Step 7: Send me a link to your landing page and I'll take a visit. I might even join your list.

Now lets move onto turning those leads into sales.

CHAPTER 11

Amplify Interest, Educate, Build Relationships

Congratulations on working through the Temptation part of your system. If you've done all the action items, you'll soon get visitors and leads who have demonstrated an interest in the area you service. Note, I didn't say they have a proven interest in your company. At least not yet. All they've told you is they have a problem or concern within the realm of your work.

Your job now changes to educating those prospective clients by bringing clarity to their problems and showing why you're the best person or business to solve them. You've heard the story that to buy from you, your customers must know, like, and trust you. This is the part of your system where you'll build that trust.

Just like in your personal life, building relationships takes on more than one form. One of the biggest mistakes I see business owners making is attempting only one modality to reach their prospects. But, that being said, one beats none, and you must start somewhere. However, eventually you should aim for 3, 4, or more.

Modalities for keeping your ideal prospects educated and engaged include:
- Email (email is still the king of the online space)
- Social Media
- Videos
- Courses
- EBooks, Reports, White Papers
- Blog
- Video Blog
- Phone calls
- Direct mail and postcards
- Text messaging / SMS
- Surveys
- And many more.

Your goal should be to use as many as possible because everyone responds differently.

Back in the 1800's, researchers noted that to make a sale, a prospect needed to be "touched" (no, I don't mean physically) or reached out to an average of 7 times. But in today's interconnected world, this number has jumped many times. Everyone is so bombarded with different messages; you need to work harder than ever to stay at the front of your customer's thoughts.

According to direct marketing expert Jerry Jones, it takes more steps than in the past to sell big-ticket items. In Direct Marketing Profit Insider (Issue 10) he says if you aren't willing to make 10, 20, or even 30 or more follow-ups, using every medium available, you're leaving money on the table, and not making as much income as you should.

Is it any wonder your sales are not as high as they could be? Are you staying in touch with your contacts for 30 touch points? Most businesses and sales reps aren't. Many I've met aren't even doing it once.

I've worked with sales reps selling 6 figure products who never follow up or only follow up one time and then whine about the quality of leads because they aren't making sales. And I'm not alone, according to statistics 48% of sales reps never follow up with prospects at all, and only 10% of sales reps make more than 3 contacts.

Quality of leads isn't the problem. Across industries, only 2% of sales are signed on the first contact, and 3% on the second. In contrast, 80% of sales are made between the 5th and 12th contact.

All you have to do to set yourself above 90% of your industry is follow up 4 or more times.

That's good news for you because after implementing and improving the Marking Automation Success System, you'll always know you're staying on top of your marketing and educating your prospects.

And once you've set up the system once, it will continue running on autopilot for years. You'll want to consistently improve it, but that's a minor commitment compared to repetitive manual outreach.

Email Marketing - Auto-responders, Broadcasts, and more.

Regardless of what social media guru's told you, email is still the king of marketing online today. The fact is, with all the junk that flies through your social news feeds daily, you're lucky if 10% even reaches your ideal customers. Anyone reading more than that's probably neglecting important tasks, things like eating and basic hygiene, so you might not want them as clients, anyway.

On the other hand, the first thing most people check in the morning and the last thing they read before bed is email. And, at a minimum, they scan every subject line.

Email is also more of a business communication channel than social media. Social media is great for sharing content, and even though it facilitates 2-way communication, it's still not as intimate or private as email. I'm not the only one who feels that way; many, many studies have proven it.

Combine email with marketing automation, and you have an unstoppable force of personalized communication, based on user activities, that runs on autopilot 24 hours per day, 7 days per week.

With marketing automation, it's not only possible to customize the email content that goes out, you can also affect which mails go out when, where the mails lead, and more. You can tag leads based on what links they clicked, increase their score or give you a notification if messages are read or forwarded, and decide exactly what products or services your ideal prospects are curious about. And their time frame to take notice.

None of this is possible with social media or any other outreach mechanism short of the telephone or face-to-face conversations. And those are far from automated.

If you want to increase revenues, and your free time, the most powerful thing your prospects can hear is "You've got mail!"

Anti Spam Legislation

Remember, in all your email marketing... Spam laws can be brutal. Under Canspam rules in the US you can be fined $16,000 for spam. The Canadian rules are even more draconian and will get you in serious hot water with maximum $1,000,000 fines for individuals, or $10,000,000 fines for corporations. While clearly insane, and potentially unenforceable legislation, it has caused many businesses to drop email marketing in Canada.

As frightening (and ridiculous) as the legislation is however, it opens a wide field of opportunity for you. The important thing is to get permission. And if possible, get permission at least twice.

Single or Double Opt In?

Now is a good point to discuss how you get permission to email your contacts and what makes up SPAM.

In the US, as a general rule, 1 on 1 email will not get you into trouble as one criterion for SPAM is that it is bulk mail.

The Canadian legislation is a lot less clear and states any electronic transmission. The law states that the mail must be "commercial" in nature. But anything you send from your business falls into that case. It might also be true inviting a friend to a network-marketing meeting (although they would be a shitty friend if they reported you).

Long story short, make sure you have permission before sending anything.

With Single Opt in mail, you are relying on one request to email information. This could be a form on your site, or could be someone giving you a business card and asking to be added to your list.

As a side note, giving you a business card DOES NOT qualify as permission, so don't just go out collecting business cards and adding everyone to your Auto-responder.

With Double Opt in, the contact is entered and the system immediately emails a confirmation. If the reader does not confirm this mail, they won't get mailed anything again, other than maybe one more reminder to confirm.

In the past, for offline consulting businesses, I recommended single opt in. Unfortunately, with double opt in, you tend to lose a percentage of your leads who never see the confirmation mail - like, for instance, if that message goes to the spam folder.

Today unfortunately, because of the stiff laws, I recommend everyone takes the punch and uses double opt in.

The key to using it successfully is making sure your offer is compelling enough your leads don't mind opting in again. And remind your readers immediately what will happen next so they know to look in their inbox.

Segmenting

One of the most rare, and also one of the most effective tools you can use to increase your email conversions is by segmenting your email list and then personalizing your mails.

According to Mailchimp, open rates increase by 14.52%, and clicks are 58.21% higher with segmented campaigns than non-segmented campaigns. And unsubscribes drop by 10.07%. Also interesting, is the number of abuse reports drops by 7.22%, and with the growth of spam protection laws this stat alone could potentially save your bottom line.

Ask yourself this question, "Would I be happier if the email I got addressed my specific situation?"

Of course. But as obvious as this is, very few businesses actually take the time to segment their lists.

Segmentation simply means splitting your list into various segments based on specific criteria. This could be something like sex, location, income, or almost any other piece of data you can get from your list.

A simple example might be a clothing company sending a mail about men's slacks to one list, and sun dresses to another.

Of course this personalization can be as broad or as specific as you like. From broad topics like whether they are active or not, right down to more specific items such as career specialty, number of kids, or products and services they have purchased in the past.

Like most parts of your system, the level of specificity and the approach you take to addressing this comes down to your business, and your strategy. If there are services you offer that certain segments would never be interested in, that would be a good place to start, and make sure you segment and only send to those who could use that service.

Auto-responders

Auto-responders make up the backbone of any good automation strategy. They are automatic mails sent, on a predetermined schedule, after the user performs some action. This action could be filling out a form - the normal way of entering your funnel - calling you on the phone, or scheduling a consultation.

They can even be used after meeting someone at an event in person, but make sure you receive confirmation they want to receive your mails in that case. Otherwise you'll be guilty of the SPAM I warned about.

After you've been in business for a while, you'll notice that most of your customers go through a specific buying path, between hearing about you the first time, and purchasing your services. Even if you have a brand new business, this buyer's path follows a consistent path across industries.

Your goal with email marketing is to inform and educate, but also to move your buyers along this predisposed path.

An Auto-responder is perfect for this because anyone who enters your business follows that same path.

The goals of auto-responders is:

1. Engage.

This is the first step, if you don't engage your readers at once, chances are they won't read any more of your mails. In engagement mails your goals is to have your readers take an easy action. These actions could be to download the report they opted in for, setting up white labeling so your emails don't go to the spam folder, or sending you an email with a question or letting you know their goals.

The action can also be going to your Facebook page and "Like"ing you so they never miss an important message -- although like I said earlier, Liking your Facebook page is no guarantee they'll get your message in their feed.

Your engagement mail should also tell the reader what they can expect to hear from you, the frequency, and anything else you want them to know.

2. Educate.

After your readers are engaged, you want to tell them who you are, what you do, and how you do it. Focus each mail on a specific problem you solve. Or give them a tip to help them in whatever area you work in.

3. Amplify their interest.

The end goals of your emails are to sell your services or move leads down the path to buying. Otherwise, you are running a hobby, not a business. At some point, you'll need to make an offer, the topic of the next chapter.

This offer doesn't have to be a buy, it can be an invitation to a webinar, a download, or to schedule a free consultation. But you will have to have a call to action if your want your Autoresponders to be successful.

With an automatic marketing system such as the ActiveCampaign or Infusionsoft software, you can take different actions depending on user interaction. For example, if they click a link in one mail, it could add them to a list with more specific details about whatever that link was referring to.

You'll also be able to see what mails your prospects read so when you follow up in person or on the phone, you have a good idea of what they do or don't know about your business. This "read" detection isn't 100% accurate, since it relies on your reader downloading a graphical pixel as part of the email, but it's better than nothing and its improving as more users read HTML mail.

Broadcast Mail

Broadcast mails are a critical part of your email arsenal. They differ from Auto-responders in they are not setup to automatically run at set intervals based on sign up. Instead they are sent only one time, and to everyone in the segment of your list you are sending mail to.

Broadcast mails can range from a monthly or weekly ezine (online magazine) to special series of mails to promote a deal, special, or affiliate product.

They offer timely information and are only sent once, so this could also include news alerts, warnings, or one time offers.

Tip: When sending broadcast mails to promote an offer, a series of 3 - 5 mails is magical. One mail for a promo is usually not enough.

How to Write Email

There are as many ways to write emails, as there are ways to write letters or any other ads. So the first thing to ask is the goal of the mail. Do you want to make an offer? Are you passing information? Is this your regular newsletter?

Regardless of the goal, you won't go wrong by remembering that for email to be effective it should be personalized. There are cases where an electronic flyer will get consumed, like a Black Friday Special. But even those are only effective when the recipient already knows, likes, and trusts you. I know I ignore flyers, and spam filters often end up dumping them unread into my trash.

Telling a story is incredibly powerful within emails. People naturally get absorbed into stories and if you can capture their imagination right away, they'll stick with you right to the end, and take the desired action. We've been conditioned throughout history to learn via stories, so even when we try, we can't ignore them.

This is especially powerful in Auto-responders and series' where you can continue a story from one mail to the next and have users glued to their in-boxes making sure they never miss another email from you. This is called opening a loop, where you open an idea in one email, and then not close it until a later mail.

The human mind doesn't like open loops. It wants to close them. So readers automatically need to know what happens next and close that loop. TV series writers are masters at this. Have you ever watched a marathon Netflix session all the way through a series?

They work just as well in your email auto-responders, sales copy, and throughout your sales funnel.

However you want to structure and word your email series, there are some goals you should keep in mind.

Introduce Your Self and Let your prospects Get to Know You

Most business owners know leads need to be nurtured before they'll buy. We've all heard stats like 50% of prospects not being ready to buy today, and 79% of leads never buying at all, thanks to a lack of nurturing. But knowing you have to nurture your leads, and actually doing it are 2 different things, as shown by many of the sequences I've seen. Unfortunately, knowing what to say is where things get more difficult.

When you're seducing a mate, you don't start with a proposal right out the gate. Instead, you entice your future bride by letting them get to know you better. Coffee, dinner and a movie, then a day frolicking in the park, a romantic weekend, etc.

When someone fills in the opt in form on your website, your approach should be the same. Don't just jump in and ask for a sale, instead, allow your new prospect to warm up to you. This process can happen quickly, but it does need to be done in order and systematically.

Immediately after a new prospect signs up to your lists, for example from your lead magnet, begin your first sequence, the "Getting to Know You" sequence. Depending on your business, goals, and the size of your service, this first sequence can be anywhere from 3 – 10 mails.

Confirm Their Interest

There's lots of discussion within the industry about double opt in mails. They've been standard in the Internet marketing industry – where spam is so prevalent – for a long time, but for service providers, they're still optional.

We've talked about spam and opt in's earlier, so we don't need to cover it again. But if you are using double opt in, it needs to be the first mail in your sequence.

Deliver the Value

The next mail in your sequence should go out right away, the minute your new prospect confirms their interest. This mail should be a simple welcome into your tribe along with a link or attachment with your bribe, or whatever you offered in the way of new information.

Note, while an attachment works, by using a link instead, you give yourself valuable intelligence into who is downloading and consuming the information. Also attachments are more likely to get blocked by spam filters, or ignored, as people are cautious about opening attachments.

In addition, by sending the prospect back to your website, you can give them further action steps like joining your Facebook group, kicking off other automations, or giving the first video in a launch style or interest building series like you'll learn in the free Automatic Entrepreneur Automatic Independence System Quick Start (http://glenkowalski.com/webcast)

It also helps psychologically because you are giving instructions to follow. This is a powerful tool in your arsenal for move prospects down the buying path.

Set Expectations

Often times, I'll combine mail 2 and 3 into one, and you might want to consider testing it both ways.

In this mail, you want to accomplish three goals.

First, remind the reader of how they subscribed to your list. And the benefits they'll receive by reading and implementing whatever information you sent.

Next, set the expectations of the frequency you'll be sending, the type of information they'll learn, and the benefits they'll receive by reading.

Treat this mail almost as a sales letter because you'll also explain how to make sure they continue receiving your mail, so you want to keep your reader engaged.

Include information on whitelisting your email address, filtering the mail into a new folder (if desired), etc.

Introduce Yourself

Now that you've done the mechanics of delivering on your first promise, and making sure the reader can receive your other mails, its time to introduce yourself. By now, your prospect has already downloaded your information, and is maybe already seeing the benefits and the value you've given them. If you've done a good job your leads will be primed to learn more about you and your work.

Think in terms of dating. In the first 3 mails, you gave value, made sure your prospect was comfortable, and the first date was setup.

In this mail, you are on the first date and letting your prospect know who you are and giving them the opportunity to learn more about you.

It's not good to be overly pushy here. You just want to let your prospect feel you out and decide if you are someone they want to learn more about.

Start Delivering Real Value

In the last mail, you showed your prospect who you were, now's your chance to deepen the relationship. Give them your best content, and the most value. Help them solve their problems and issues. Enhance their lives or businesses because of what you have to offer.

This is your perfect opportunity to really use the open loops you learned about early to keep your readers opening your mails. In a launch style funnel, this is where you'll drive your readers to later videos, webcasts, etc.

Be generous, you'll spend much of your time in this part of the series. Many service providers are scared if they give their best value, the client won't hire them.

But talk to most successful coaches and consultants and you'll hear the opposite is true. The service providers who give the most up front are the ones your clients will work with in the future.

Show How You can help

By this time, your prospect has learned who you are and what you stand for. They've had a chance to experience how generous you are and seen your expertise in action.

They may not be quite ready to buy yet, but its time you let them know you are capable of helping solve their most dire issues.

You're also setting them up to offer products and / or services in the future.

Up to this point, everything you have sent in your mails has been about letting the potential or new client get to know, like, and trust you. It's kind of like a first date.

But just like when you're dating, you don't want to stay in the friend zone forever. You want to move the relationship to the next level, or you are wasting your time.

So if you haven't been pitching yet, you have to. But you might be wondering what to write about.

Ask yourself, "What is the main topic or deliverable of the lead magnet they used to sign up to your list?"

That'll give you your answer. You want to be writing your engagement series about the topic of your lead magnet. What concerns did your lead magnet address? What solutions does it offer?

Talk specifically about the problems your clients face, and the solutions you offer, based on the lead magnet they downloaded.

For example, what if your lead magnet was "The Top 5 Ways to Save Money on Your Taxes This Year?" You know your prospect is working or own a business, and you know they make enough money they're paying significant taxes on it. And you know they want to save money on taxes. So tell your prospect how your solution will help them reduce taxes. And then ask for the sale.

The length of your engagement series depends on the dollar value of what you are selling. In general, they'll start around 3 emails for an inexpensive introductory offer. And they could go for several mails for a high-end product or service.

Most times though, you won't see an engagement series last longer than 30 days. If they haven't responded to your offer within that time frame, it's time to start considering another offer.

One of my favorite email campaigns for this selling or engagement series comes via Digital Marketer and is called the Gain / Logic / Fear campaign. It's extremely powerful because it addresses all the major purchase triggers your prospect experiences.

Think about it...

Any time you buy anything it's to gain what the purchase offers, because it logically makes sense, or because you're scared of the result if you don't.

Here's how it works

Establish the Gain

The first mail of the engagement series goes out immediately after your get to know you mails. It should point to a gain your prospect will get from purchasing your service or offer. For consultants, this is often a free discovery or strategy session. Yes, I said free, but because the client is offering you up 30 minutes or an hour of their time, it's still considered a sale.

Your mail should remind the client of the big gain they were looking for when they downloaded your lead magnet. And prove the gain they'll get by working with you.

Appeal to Their Logic

Show your prospect why it makes sense to take you up on your offer from a logic standpoint. For example, "Obviously you're interested in living abroad, or you wouldn't have downloaded the {x} report. You already know it takes a plan to pack your bags and get going, so why not take us up on our free <u>Pick the Destination of Your Dreams Session?</u> It only makes sense..."

Lay out the Fear

Make the prospect realize they will regret not taking you up on your offer. Remind them of the potential gains, but only enough so they fear losing those. One-way is with scarcity, but only if your offer is really scarce.

If not, one strategy is to tell the prospect this is the last time you'll mention {your offer}. And make sure it is.

"Hey, this is the last time I'll tell you about our free 'Have the best year ever' break out session, so take us up on it now."

After that, if they don't "buy", move the prospect on to other lists, angles, or offers, but don't keep presenting this exact offer.

The Gain / Logic / Fear is only one example email engagement series for this phase of your auto-responder, but it's a powerful one that works in almost any niche. Remember this section of your series is where you'll begin selling your products, services, free consultations, etc.

But remember, after your first date, it's time to move the relationship to the next level. The same is true in your email auto-responder sequence. You want to move out of the friend zone and actually create a sale or move your prospect down the buyers funnel.

Grow Your Relationship

No one dreams of staying stuck in an affair floating into an abyss. You know, trapped in the friend zone in a mind numbingly dull relationship where you give and give and give, but never get anything in return. But, enough about my past dating life...

The point of relationships is to grow and develop until both parties satisfy the need they got into the partnership to achieve.

If you accept that truth (and you should), why do most business owners treat marketing like buying dinners for hundreds of different love interests? But never turn it into a relationship? Uh oh, flash backs again...

When the relationship with your lead, prospect, or customer started, it was because they had an urgent need that your lead magnet helped to fulfill. And if you followed the steps in email series two, the engagement series, many of your prospects bought your tripwire or core product as a bigger solution to that need. But have you fulfilled their ultimate want?

Is your client where they dreamed of being when you first encountered them? Or, have you solved one pain, but left others aching for a cure?

Most times, one product or service won't solve all your clients' ultimate needs. They can usually make more money, get into better shape, enjoy life more, or do more of whatever you sell.

For example, if you're a love coach, maybe you helped your client get a date. But their real goal isn't a date, it's getting married. Your aim should be to ascend your client further towards that ultimate need.

This is true for almost every service imaginable, get creative.

Be Creative and Personal

Above all your emails should be creative, personal, and engaging. Tell stories, ask questions, and get your readers involved. Email still is the king of engagement, so spend time making sure yours is the best it can be.

Automating Email

In Infusionsoft, Auto-responder mails are created via campaigns. In ActiveCampaign it is done via automations.

Creating one is simply a matter of creating a campaign for a specific list and then adding emails with set intervals between them. You can also direct various paths, or start and stop this sequence or others, depending on activity.

For an Auto-responder, I recommend starting with at least 7-10 emails. These can be sent daily or at any interval you specify. 3 days is a good benchmark because any longer than that, and your prospect has time to forget you, and / or the email story you were telling.

Remember earlier we said prospects need minimum of 7 touch points? An auto-responder gives you ample opportunities to offer a free consultation, program, webinar, course, or other product or service.

Speaking of which, most companies use emails, both Auto-responders and broadcast mails, to engage with new prospects. But don't forget your existing clients -- your best source of referrals and further sales. Many companies forget about this group entirely, but you know better. You can set up a trigger when your prospect becomes a client to put them into another Auto-responder series to keep them engaged.

Or, you could have a trigger when one project completes, to warm your client to other services you offer. Or you could offer post project support, over delivering and keeping you at the front of their minds.

The options are endless.

CHAPTER 12

Content Marketing Strategies

In addition to your emails, there is a multitude of ways to keep your prospects engaged through the power of content. Content marketing also has the added benefits of improving your search engine optimization and your temptation system in general.

And fortunately, much of it can be automated so you get the benefits with little ongoing time commitment.

Blog

The blog is the foundation of most company's content marketing strategy. It's a chance to educate and inform your prospects and clients about topics of interest to them.

To be successful, your blog should be informational, not hype. It should have a call to action in most cases. But the action your reader takes doesn't have to always be buying your product or service.

There are exceptions to every rule, and some blog posts make a direct pitch. But this should be the exception.

Your blog posts can be automated with several editorial calendar plugins. Also, there are several services allowing you to hire writers and automatically post unique content at a specific date.

Video Blog

A video blog is like a blog and follows many of the same rules. The difference is, with a video blog you are talking into a camera instead of typing words on the page.

You can use YouTube, Video, or a wide variety of other platforms to host pre-recorded videos. For even more engagement, you can use Google Hangouts, Periscope, Blab, or Meerkat, or others in the growing family of video streaming services.

Podcasts

Another avenue for content delivery that's becoming more popular is podcasts. Like the blog and the video blog, it centers on information, not sales. Prospects can subscribe to your channel to learn more about the types of problems you solve.

Newsletter

We covered the newsletter above when we talked about broadcast mails. But just be aware it is another content strategy you should be employing, and it is easy to automate the delivery and analysis.

Note: Many businesses use newsletters as a lead magnet. They are not lead magnets. By all means, use a "Sign up for my newsletter" form on your website, but understand newsletters are different from lead magnets, and you still need one of those.

EBooks, Reports, and Whitepapers

In addition to making excellent lead magnets for your attraction strategy, reports, eBooks and whitepapers can educate your tribe and pull them closer to making a deal with your company.

Just because you already have your contacts information is no reason to stop giving information in this format.

Surveys

Surveys may not seem like content since they are more about you engaging your prospects and clients and asking them for feedback. So while they are important for that use, and you should use them to help plan your content strategy, the results they produce become excellent content on their own as other prospective clients will have an interest in the same topics.

Social Media

Facebook, Twitter, YouTube, LinkedIn, and about a million other social media channels are available and just waiting for you to publish content. These tools work best to engage prospects and drive them back to your website which should be the hub of your marketing.

This is another area where you don't want to try dominating every choice. Instead of freeing up your time you'll be pulled into an endless void of time sucking hell. But used properly as a publishing tool, and with the right automation tools in place, like Hootsuite, you'll soon find your prospects consuming your content more than ever.

Online Courses

Online education is becoming more popular and is gradually replacing info marketing and many other content channels people use to learn about subjects interesting to them.

Online education bridges the gap between information, and learning and has a higher perceived value, more accountability (through quizzes, etc.), and makes an excellent content channel in addition to a brand new revenue stream.

Webinars and Webcasts

Webinars and webcasts are a favorite education / amplification channel that is working for all types of businesses. I have a free training on webinars and webcasts you can sign up for at http://glenkowalski.com/webcast

Other Content Channels

The world of content marketing keeps expanding and there will always be new channels opening. From press releases to guest posts to Web TV shows and more, content creation is an area that keeps getting more exciting.

The most important thing to remember with content marketing is consistency. Don't try making an impact in all areas. Start with one or two and update at least weekly. If there's anything worse than not having a blog at all, its having a blog that isn't updated regularly with new content.

Just as new content channels come online all the time, there will also be new ways to automate this content creation and delivery. There are many tools for automating blog posts, social media updates, and drip-feeding all types of content already. So if you're looking to automate your marketing, you'll want to keep your eyes open.

Action Steps

Action Step 1: Create an email Auto-responder that will go out on a regular basis when someone signs up for your lead capture offer you created in the last chapter.

Action Step 2: Add this series to your marketing automation system and test it.

Action Step 3: Create a content marketing plan. You can download a template from http://glenkowalski.com/contentplan

Action Step 4: Start your content strategy. At a minimum, you should consider a monthly newsletter and a weekly blog post. But also consider videos and podcasts.

Action Step 5: Sign up for my free webcast training at http://glenkowalski.com/webcast.

CHAPTER 13

Make an Offer

Education, nurturing, and amplifying interest are great. But if you're in business to make money, and you want to feed your family, enjoy travel, or do whatever it is you dream of doing in your spare time, eventually you'll have to make an offer and sell something. You got practice with making an offer in the temptation part of the system. In that case, you traded a small bit of value for an email address.

But now, you're looking for a bigger commitment. You're looking to trade value for money, or in some cases, a commitment of time and effort.

Types of Offers

The Low Dollar and / or Higher Time Commitment Offer

Ryan Deiss call this a tripwire. I've also heard it called welcome mat.

The theory behind a "tripwire" or low price offer is that the easiest sale you'll ever make, is to an existing customer, so you want to make it easy to become a customer. We'll talk more about that in chapter 12. But for now it's enough to understand that selling to existing customers is much easier than selling to a customer the first time. With new customers, you have the highest customer acquisition costs because of marketing, advertising, etc.

For that reason, you want to make the transition from lead to customer as frictionless as possible. And turn as many prospects as you can into customers.

When you are dealing with a potential client who's never worked with you, do you think it's easier to sell a $10 product, or a $10,000 service?

Exactly. The $10 product, as long as it solves a tangible need, or moves your client down the path towards their goals; it's almost a no brainer. Most people will snap it up.

But the mental shift that's made at that point is monumental.

From this point on when you make offers to this individual you aren't talking to a cold prospect. You're talking to a valued client or friend. The importance of this mindset shift can't be overstated.

This low-ticket sale is known as a tripwire, introductory offer, or welcome mat.

Ryan Deiss, CEO of one of the largest digital marketing companies on the planet, is where I first heard the term tripwire. The name tripwire comes from a type of booby trap where a thin wire is laid out across the path. Anyone walking along the path will trip over the wire, at which point the predator or enemy has the advantage and can move in for the kill.

This somewhat negative connotation has prompted some people to call it the nicer term of welcome mat or introductory offer (which is boring as hell as a title).

Whatever you call it though, the idea behind it is the same.

You are making it an incredibly easy, almost impulse, decision to become a customer.

For most offline businesses though - companies outside of the Internet marketing space -- There's a better approach.

You can get the same or close to the same benefits of the low ticket offer by giving away something free, but instead asking for a time commitment.

As a service provider, a good example of a welcome mat offer would be a free consultation, webinar, or discovery session. Your prospect isn't paying you in dollars. But they are giving you a time commitment in exchange for the value you're delivering. This makes the lead a customer since they have paid you something for something else.

Once this transaction has taken place, your relationship is different. They're no longer just a cold lead. Now the prospect is a client, since they have, in fact, learned from you. You have provided a service.

I'd be remiss if I didn't mention one of the reasons tripwires are losing some of their appeal. As competition increases, so do paid advertising costs. That means making low price tripwire offers "pay" off from cold traffic in many industries is getting more difficult. When you're selling a $10,000 product it becomes a moot point, but it is something to be aware of. There are solutions, but they are advanced funnels and outside of simple lead generation and industry / product specific.

When to make the First Offer

When you present your first offer will vary based on your industry and services but it should normally be offered right after the lead has received the lead magnet.

As a rule, you'll offer the low ticket and / or higher commitment item immediately after your new lead downloads the lead magnet you created in chapter 7. For example, right on the thank you page you could say something like "Congratulations, your Report is on the way to your email box. Before going there though, I have a very special offer to tell you about..." and then lead them into enrolling in a free discovery session or webinar.

You'll also offer this item as part of the follow-up Autoresponder you created in chapter 8. You can offer your core product or service in those mails, but you'll often get more mileage and success if you start with your lower ticket offer.

Another spot a low ticket / time commitment item is useful is as part of your loop back / follow up you'll discover in chapter 12.

In this case you are marketing to existing clients, but want to introduce them to a completely new service offering. For example, if you have a global banking product, you could introduce them to international trusts. By starting them with a low-ticket trust report you're inserting them into another sales pipeline and have bypassed the lead magnet attraction phase because they are already your customers.

Core Offer(s)

For most service providers, their "core offer" is well known to them. It is their flagship product, the main service they offer. In other words, you are selling it for a dollar amount, not just a commitment. And ideally you are actually making money from it.

Notice I said "ideally" and I said "some" money. This was intentional because in the Internet marketing space, most of your money is made after your core offer, and the goal of many marketers is to break even at the core offer stage. For coaches, consultants, and service providers though, I think this gets too complex and forces you to spend too much time at the top of your funnel. At the core offer stage, you should be selling whatever service you got into business to sell. And you should be making money on it.

When to Make Your Offer and Lead Scoring

When you have a busy sales team, even if that sales team consists of just you, its vital you spend time on the prospects most likely to buy at the time. All the work you have done to this point culminates in getting the data to know exactly the right time to present your leads with an offer.

This is what lead scoring is all about. You can assign relative scores to various activities your leads perform so you can see at a glance the hottest leads. For example, you could assign one star or flame for downloading a report.

Or 2 stars for sitting all the way through a webinar, or calling you on the phone.

Your automation software will take care of all of this administration for you automatically. You just need to set it up the first time by including a step in your campaigns to add the correct number based on the weighted value of an activity.

Both Infusionsoft and ActiveCampaign make this easy, as do most other automation suites. After a step is completed in a campaign, or after a goal is reached, just add the value.

Action Steps

Action Step 1: Visit the automated follow up sequences you created in the amplification step, and add a star for downloading the report, and another for reaching the end of your follow-up sequence without unsubscribing.

Action Step 2: Decide on other criteria you could use for scoring which leads are hot and where you should spend your time.

Back End Offers

We'll cover back end offers more in a later chapter. They deserve a chapter of their own because back end offers are where the money is made. It's been said that the company who can spend the most money to acquire a customer wins. Back end offers allow you to spend the entire profits of your core offer on acquiring new customers and driving your competitors right out of the market.

It's why Amazon is successful. It's how Agora can make almost 1 billion dollars as a financial publisher when their core offerings start at 49 bucks.

What Is Your Offer

Have you ever asked yourself what you're really offering?

Oh sure, maybe its tax advice or Bitcoin training, or one of a million other descriptions everyone in your industry is using.

But for service providers, no one cares about what you do. And usually not even how you do it, although that comes into play in your copy. What they care about is what results you offer.

All of your marketing, copywriting, and branding should be geared at showing your ideal client how you can help them.

Do you solve a specific problem? That makes a great headline. Will you save them $19,492 on their taxes? Great, sign me up.

You need to summarize and sexy up the problems you solve, and what results you clients will see when they implement your service.

Launch Your Core Service

According to Jeff Walker, the guy best known for product launches in the online marketing space, how you launch your product can be the difference between failure and a million dollar product.

Obviously if you are already running a business, it's too late to launch your core product. Or is it?

While your existing clients already know what you do, you have scores of new fans that have no idea. Many businesses run a perpetual launch, where you launch like you are starting a brand new service, but only to new people in your sphere or brand new leads. This can be an excellent way to introduce your new leads to what you do, especially for higher end services.

In addition as you add new products and services to your line, those can be sent out as a launch as well.

A launch can be as simple or as complex as you want. But to use a launch to free up more of your time and skyrocket your revenues, you'll want to plan it out and automate the entire process.

A multi-step launch includes several pieces of content in various modalities. Usually it will include several videos and automatic broadcast mails to move your lead down the buyer's path. The most common formula today, is a series of 3 videos that give killer content about a big problem your service solves. You will then follow up by a video sales letter selling your product.

In between each video an automatic email follow up sequence guides your leads to the next video.

For service providers this process can be useful if you offer a course, and can also be useful for group coaching programs. For individual clients it can be powerful for high end coaching programs. Because of the amount of work involved in creating these launches, if you have a small list, the perpetual launch might be a more cost effective choice. Once its setup once, it will run on autopilot forever.

You can also scale it back with a series of emails instead of videos, or with a single webinar - a super tool to sell your services.

Think of it as a mini system within a system.

If you want to learn more about product launches, I recommend you check out Jeff's book on Amazon or his full launch program online.

To see a sample of a webcast funnel setup like a perpetual launch, visit http://glenkowalski.com/webcast.

Action Steps

Action Step: Create sales pages for your introductory and core offers and hook them up to your automation system. At a minimum make sure you are tagging your clients to know what they've purchased.

Action Step 2: If you have an automatic sales page (which we'll talk about more in the next chapter) setup any notifications you need to fulfill the purchase.

Action Step 3: Think about how you can create either a one time or perpetual launch of your flagship product.

CHAPTER 14

Close the Deal

Now you've made an offer designed to be perfect for your ideal clients and your leads are busting down your doors to buy your core offer. But just because your leads need what you're selling, or even expressed interest, doesn't mean the deal will close.

And when / if the deal closes, if you want to set yourself up for success for back-end sales, referrals, and bigger deals, that closing process needs to be smooth and professional.

This means having every person in your company, along with your automated and manual processes setting the tone for a closing process that works. Automation lets you do this because you're informed the minute the offer is made and your lead is "hot."

Do you have a closing process?

It's surprising the number of businesses that don't. Even if they're working and collecting an income, there's no process in place, and no automated systems. So they're wasting time they should use to grow their business (or hang on the beach). And they're not growing as fast as they could or leaving money on the table.

According to the Baymard Institute, approximately 68.63% of sales online result in an abandoned cart. I've heard different statistics, but the moral of the story is many people who almost buy, end up not buying.

These are potential clients who've expressed an interest in your product or service, but then changed their mind. Since most people didn't change the fundamental reason they thought of buying that quickly, the more likely scenario is they got confused, didn't know what to do next, or something happened in the checkout process that reduced their trust.

Maybe the entire closing process seemed like too much effort. For example, if you need a wire transfer of funds and / or don't accept credit cards.

While your service business might not accept online payments, it's still important to pay attention to the items discussed in this chapter, as they'll cover both online and offline techniques, tools, and tactics in collecting money.

Because face it, if you aren't collecting your payment, everything you've done to this point is a waste of time. This system is designed around creating time and income. Don't blow it when you're this close.

Abandoned Carts

Before we move on to discussing actual closing procedures, since we're discussing cart abandonment, here's one system any company that accepts payment online should start as soon as possible. **A cart abandonment campaign.**

As the name implies, cart abandonment is a specific campaign that runs whenever someone makes it as far as your cart, but then doesn't continue with the purchase.

Here, you should send out at least 3 mails. In the first mail, you could assume that the lead got interrupted, and politely remind them to continue with their purchase.

In the second, you might assume they got confused, and walk through the steps to completing the purchase successfully.

And in the third, you should ask the customer outright why they didn't finish. Sure, most people won't answer you, but the ones that do will give you a wealth of knowledge you couldn't buy for any price.

Just implementing the abandoned cart campaign to your success system could save you as many as 50% of the cart abandonments. How much would that be worth to your bottom line? You might need to wait to hook your campaign up to your invoicing system, but there's no reason to wait before writing your sequence you know you'll need if you accept payments online.

Action Steps

Action Step 1: Create a series of 3 mails you'll send if someone abandons a shopping cart before completing the purchase.

Sales Process

Earlier in this book we talked about your sales pipeline. This is the process your leads and prospects move through the path to becoming a customer. This is one process. But that high-level process isn't enough. You need systems in place that give a roadmap to a smooth and professional close.

This closing process includes clear documentation you give to your new clients, terms and conditions, contracts and work agreements, receipts, and more. The process should outline what happens next, and what your customer can expect as you deliver on the promise you're delivering.

For many service providers, it includes clear onboarding steps, and who is responsible to complete each one. It will also include things like warrantees, deeds of ownership, contracts, and more.

Invoicing and Collecting Payment

How easy is it for your clients to send payments to you? This means ease for you and your clients. Do you have to haul a check to the bank and wait 14 days for it to clear? What about international checks, can you even accept them? Do your clients have to wire you money via Western Union or their bank? Or can they use a credit card?

Have you opened a PayPal or other merchant account so your prospects can pay via credit card? If so, have you thought about chargebacks?

And what about presenting invoices and receipts? Is this an easy automatic process? Or are you writing receipts by hand and then spending hours transferring it into your accounting system? If you haven't lost the manual paper work first.

Just by having an automatic invoicing system, especially one that's hooked up to your merchant account, you'll save hours every month by automating the process of collecting money.

One advantage of Infusionsoft is its built in invoicing system is automatically tied to your CRM for record tracking and kicking off automation and campaigns. But if you don't want to be stuck using Infusionsoft's invoicing, your can tie your ActiveCampaign to WooCommerce, the largest e-selling platform on the web and get the same (or more) power. That way you have the power of the best in breed commerce solution while using the easy to use automation system you've already setup.

Imagine if the minute a client accepts a proposal or quote from you, they automatically receive an invoice. Once they've paid the invoice, they receive an email with your terms of conditions, and a form to fill out to use for your on-boarding procedures.

Your customer gets to do this anytime, day or night. And you haven't lifted a finger at all. Your fulfillment team (or you) is automatically notified the purchase went through so you are ready with any next steps you need to take.

Or take it one step further, once the payment is accepted, your client could be redirected to a page where they pick their own appointment slots for your first meeting. You simply have to let the system know your availability, and it magically presents all your free slots for your client to pick one.

Both you and your client receive calendar updates and email reminders so neither of you are late nor miss the appointment. And this happens behind the scenes without you or an expensive assistant handling the workflow.

Employee Training

It's not enough to commit to writing these processes. All the processes in the world won't free up your time or increase your revenue if your employees don't understand and follow them. Fortunately, with your automation system in place, that's easy to enforce.

All you or your staff needs to do is email an invoice. This can happen by moving your client's deal or opportunity status to something like an "Invoice Sent" status. Then once the invoice is paid, the system automatically moves the client into the closed stage, kicking off the automation. Infusionsoft, by design will not update the status automatically. But your automation system will send the sales rep a notification so he can make the move manually.

If your invoicing isn't tied to your automation system for whatever reason, your sales rep just has to move the client along when he receives notification of payment. The entire process takes seconds.

Action Steps

Action Step 1: If appropriate, setup your online invoicing system using either WooCommerce or built in Infusionsoft invoicing. There are ample help documents available for each one.

Action Step 2: Write out your closing process. What documents do you need? And in what order? What steps need to happen when the customer is ready to buy? If any new documentation is required, get it created and ready as soon as possible.

Action Step 3: Setup your automation system to email required documents and create notifications for your sales reps, fulfillment teams, clients, and anyone else who needs anything in a repeatable way.

Congratulations, you've now built out systems to attract leads into your business and a system for selling your product. If you stopped here, you're already in a position for growth and freeing up hours of your time every month to spend time on those things that matter. Instead of repeated processes that are critical but don't add value to your life.

But, I know you're better than that, and you won't stop. In the next 3 chapters, you'll increase your customer's lifetime value by turning them into loyal repeat buyers who'll not only buy more often and bigger services, but refer their friends and colleagues to your company. And you'll see your revenues soar in ways you always aspired to, but never seemed able to reach.

CHAPTER 15

Over Deliver and Wow

Now you're finally collecting money and you can take a deep breath because things are always easier when money is coming through the door. But you can't rest on your laurels just yet. You're a service provider, and not the person who just collects the money and runs.

At least, I hope you're not.

You still have to deliver on your promise.

Your main business is delivering your service, and it's what you do well. So delivery might seem like a no brainer for you. But these days, delivering isn't enough. Especially if you want to take your business to the next level of income by having your customers purchase bigger services. And refer you to their friends.

For those to happen, you need to delight and wow your customers. You can't just have them satisfied, but ecstatic to have worked worth you, and clawing at the walls to work with you again.

Fortunately, thanks to the Unconventional Entrepreneur Automatic Marketing System, you can provide that wow factor while still giving yourself more free time, more money, and more vacation. Sounds like a great recipe for success.

Delivery

How you deliver your service will depend on what type of service you offer. And the core package your client purchased. But almost every business will enjoy having a set process in place that automatically moves the process along.

Once the user either buys the service on your website, or signs a contract and gives you a check, the customer's deal or opportunity should be moved to Won. When this happens, you'll kick off a new fulfillment or delivery campaign.

This campaign might start with a notification to you, and another one to your client, setting up an appointment online. If they miss your meeting, you could follow up a day or 2 later with another email. And if that doesn't get results, set a task for you to follow up on the phone.

In addition, you can automatically email any intake forms or on boarding information your client needs before your initial meeting. And give your clients an easy, automated way to get the documents back to you when they're done filling them out.

You can also send reminders and task notifications if those forms aren't filled out in a timely manner.

If your product or service contains digital files, you can send the client a link to download the information. A better option, depending on your business, might be to send them to a password protected membership area to download their files.

The advantage of a membership area is it lets your clients know they are now part of an exclusive club. It raises the level of perceived professionalism in your brand at the same time. Your membership area can also automatically drip content like homework or information at specific intervals to keep your clients engaged and learning more.

If, on the other hand, you sell physical products, you can email a list to your fulfillment team so the products are sent in the mail without delay.

After Sales Service (The Wow Factor)

With the automatic delivery systems setup above, your client is will already feel impressed with your level of service and professionalism. Most businesses they've worked with have had a half hazard product delivery system. While yours worked smoothly and professionally and allowed you the free time you need to do your best work.

But what you do after the sale can make all the difference in whether your clients will buy more or bigger services (discussed in the next chapter), or refer you to their friends (Chapter 13).

There are many things you can do after a sale to make your services stand out, it's sad so few businesses extend the effort. This important step is often missed because owners and staff are too busy with other tasks and these things just get dropped. With automation, you'll never have to worry about wowing your customers again.

For example, the least you can do is send a thank you note after you provide your service or fulfill your shipment. If you send it in email, it'll take no time and go out automatically when needed.

If you want a more personal touch, you can send out a little hand written postcard in the mail. Yes, this will take a little more manual effort, but your automation system can set you a task reminder so this critical wow generating strategy never gets missed or forgotten.

You can also get task reminders to make personal follow-up phone calls or send text messages automatically. If you're interested, there are even voice services that will make phone calls for you. I'm not a fan, but with the correct business and the correct services, this can be very effective.

What about on your client's birthdays or other special occasions? Why not send out an e-card or personalized card? Or coupons of interest to your ideal prospects.

If you sell physical products, you could have specialized packaging made that makes you stand out, or include flyers, thank you cards, catalogs, or coupons right in the box. Thanks to your automatic fulfillment list, your team will never forget to add those little extras.

Follow Up Emails

We discussed follow-up emails and Auto-responders in a previous chapter, and then come up again in the next one. But little extras you could add would be automatic mails in a month or 6 weeks to ask how your client did with the solution you provided. Or if you're a coach, to keep them accountable to decisions they made.

Going the extra mile doesn't have to be difficult or take time away from your already busy schedule. It takes creativity and a way to make the delivery automatic, so you never forget and make your time as efficient as possible. That extra personal touch, without the personal time, can differentiate between a single sale, and multiple or bigger deals. And result in raving fans for your company.

Action Steps

Action Step 1: Design and Create a delivery system for any digital downloads or forms your clients will need when receiving your service.

Action Step 2: Setup automatic reminders, mails requesting setting up an appointment, and the appointment services you need.

Action Step 3: Setup a secure membership area if appropriate for your business. Hint, most businesses find these useful, but few are using them.

Action Step 4: Send out an automatic "Welcome" mail when your clients purchase your services (either online or manually), and another automatic mail when your service is completed.

CHAPTER 16

Loop Back and Offer More

If you think making money is a good thing, your loop back mechanism or follow-up system, often called a return path, will astound you. Because up sells, cross sells, and new offers are where really successful businesses make their biggest profits. In fact, in some cases, this is where they make all of their profits.

According to Perry Belcher, a top direct marketing copywriter, it's never been more difficult to sell to a new client than today. Proliferation of advertising across the Internet and other channels has raised peoples BS detectors so high trust is next to impossible to attain. On the other hand, there's never been an easier time in history to sell to existing clients for many of the same reasons.

Most business owners and sales reps spend all of their time banging their heads against brick walls, chasing down new leads, and then as soon as someone buys from them they forget that person and go looking for new brick walls. This is inefficient when your best customers are already in your CRM and just waiting to be reactivated. And especially when that reactivation can be kicked off automatically and run on autopilot.

I've worked with clients who have sold 20K - 1MM dollar products and never follow up after the initial sale. We've implemented simple follow up, and the response is amazing.

You've likely heard the terms up sell, down sell, and cross sell, and you may have also heard of follow ups, return paths or profit maximizers and this might all sound confusing. But setting up automation to handle these types of transactions can be remarkably simple with automation tools and commerce solutions like WooCommerce.

They can be offered either immediately upon a purchase. Or via a loop back mechanism, you can offer these features via automatic emails that are sent after the purchase, or after you fulfill the service.

To get the most traction, it's wise to use as many of these as possible. But you don't want to be pushy or rude. We'll discuss a few best practices later in the chapter. Before we get into those though, we should discuss terminology and definitions.

Up Sells

Up sells are offers to increase the level of service your client has already purchased. These usually work best immediately after the purchase, but they can also be used later in the delivery cycle. Up sells should be related to the primary offer but should add to it, not be required.

For example, you promise your client your magic diet pill will make them lose weight, and then when they buy you tell them that without this second pill the first one will likely kill them. This is an unfair marketing trick I see used way too often and is more of a bait and switch than an up sell.

A better, more ethical version of an up sell is making a promise that your marketing system will increase revenues. Then the up sell can be a software package that automates the system for them. And then another up sell could be a done for you system where someone implements the software and the entire strategy for you.

WooCommerce has several add-ins that will handle immediate up sells, and there are add-ons in the Infusionsoft marketplace that'll do the same.

Down Sells

Down sells are usually offered immediately when a prospect says "no" to either your primary product or service, or an up sell attempt. These work best if they are a stripped-down version of the original service.

For example, if you are a web designer you could offer to build a new site for $1000. If the prospect says no, immediately offer to install Wordpress and give them a premium theme so they can build their own for $200.00.

The same example could be done with an Auto-responder after a failed sales attempt or abandoned cart. For example you could email saying, "We noticed you didn't complete your purchase. We understand investing $1000 might seem a little much at this time. We still want to see you successful though, so we'd like to set up Wordpress and give you an amazing theme for only $200.00 which will get you on the path to your business goals..."

Cross Sells

Cross sells involve offering different related, or possibly unrelated products to your customers. These will usually be in the same niche as the core service you sold, but unnecessary for the success of that system.

The best example of cross selling comes from Amazon. The minute you buy a book, or other product, they'll immediately show you a bunch of other items that others in your niche have bought.

For example a fitness coach could offer a strength-training plan to a weight loss client. A lawyer setting up an offshore corporation might also offer to create a trust.

As a service provider, I believe cross sells work best after your primary service is completed, or at least after you've been working with the client for a while. In most cases, it'll appear sleazy trying to pawn off other products or packages after you've just sold your client on a product that's the answer to all their dreams.

This makes cross sells ideal for the follow up sequence.

Subscriptions / Reoccurring Sales

What's better than selling your prospects a product or service? Selling them a product or service every month. Membership clubs, subscriptions, retainers, and other monthly services allow you to build reoccurring income into your business without continuing to market.

For your clients, it gives them ongoing, growing, and consistent support on the issues they need to ascend their lives and / or businesses.

Super Premium Products and Services

Super Premium products and services far above what you normally offer and that most of your prospects will not take advantage of, but because you've already paid the customer acquisition costs for this client, can be extremely profitable.

For example you run a body shop that has a paint package for $1495. You then offer a set of gold rims for $10,000 a wheel.

A more realistic example might be the lawyer selling an offshore corporation. They might offer an ultra-expensive full asset protection structure including accounts, tax shelters, banks, and more. Most clients won't need that level of protection but for the 1% ultra-wealthy it might be just what they are looking for.

I define these as super premium because, in my opinion, many if not most service providers should focus on high-end premium products as opposed to lower priced entry-level products.

But What if You Don't Sell Other Products?

Many coaches, consultants, lawyers, realtors, service providers, and other experts get hooked up on the fact they only have one or 2 products. So they don't have anything else to sell during the ascension series. I have good news, at this stage, the prospect is already your customer and in your list, so it doesn't need to be your product.

Your only goal is to grow your customer to their ideal result. So the next service can be an affiliate product, joint venture, or any other opportunity to add new products to your line.

You can develop your own new products, but other options are licensing, buying out someone else's line, wholesaling, etc.

If you want to grow your business, never let your ideal customers find the solutions they need from a competitor. Or soon you'll find they're going to that competitor for all their needs.

According to Dan Kennedy, we should always be ascending our clients. In other words just because someone has bought from you before is no reason to stop marketing to them.

Every time your client buys from you, you should put them into another series that moves them up their satisfaction ladder, until they buy your next product or service. Just like in a dating relationship, this becomes a giant feedback loop where your relationship continually grows stronger, and so does the level of results your client sees.

What if Your Prospects Don't Buy and or Go Cold?

What is Cold?

It depends on your market, but cold could be anywhere from 60 to 90 days without opening, clicking, or engaging with your mail.

Many marketer's ego's force them to focus only on list size and they don't think about this dead weigh since they figure everything's automated. But problems with non-engaged subscribers go way beyond ego.

If people living on your list aren't engaged, your list health deteriorates. In fact, because ISP's track open rates, it can even affect your deliverability and reputation.

The bottom line is, you must take an active part dealing with these unengaged readers.

Step 1 – Try to get them Re-engaged.

Your primary goal should be to place these prospects back into a new series that's providing value and selling different services.

That way they'll receive your marketing and other materials and continue being led through your funnel.

If they still won't engage after 2 or 3 mails, it's time to ask why.

Step 2 – Ask if everything is OK.

Ask your prospect if everything is ok. Ask if they are getting your emails. Ask if they're enjoying them or if there's anything you can do differently. This mail should be a friendly nudge hoping to pull a response. Use a personal tone, text only preferably, since its possible they haven't been able to read your mails, and that's why they aren't engaging. Try to get them to recommit and tell you they want to continue hearing from you.

If that doesn't spark interest after two mails, step it up a little.

Step 3 – Ask if you've offended them, or done anything wrong.

This is like the last mail you sent, but more passive aggressive. This mail will be direct, but stay personal.

"Hey Bob, I noticed you haven't been reading our emails. Have I offended you?"

If this doesn't elicit response you can assume they are no longer interested, but should give them one more chance to experience your awesomeness.

Step 4 – Send a Final Warning or Two.

Your prospect hasn't engaged with you for 60 – 90 days. They aren't answering your questions. So it's **almost** safe to assume they no longer want to see your messages. But you want to give them one or maybe 2 more warnings.

Tell them you don't want to show up as a stalker or spammer. And if they don't show they're interested in talking to you, you'll remove them from your list.

Ideally, in this last ditch effort, you'll get them to re-opt into one of your other auto-responder sequences.

Step 5 – Drop them.

Yes, it's painful. And yes, I'm guessing you'd rather not. But because of the reasons discussed above, you need to remove these prospects from your list. If you can't make yourself do that, move them to a different email server and provider. Spam them from that list if you want, but continuing to send from your main list will damage your reputation.

It hurts, but it has to be done.

Having an unengaged list is worse than not having a list at all. Each name on your list costs you money, and non-responsive subscribers hurt your deliverability to prospects who want to hear from you.

CHAPTER 17

The Loop Back Mechanism

The loop back is a series of touch points, usually email, designed to keep your existing clients engaged, and give them other offers.

How you structure your loop back depends on what other services you offer and your business model. But it is the primary vehicle you'll use to reactivate clients you've either stopped working with, or have been working with for a while.

You can also send your clients back to an earlier stage in a funnel or pipeline. For example, send them to a landing page for another service they may be interested in. Once they buy, download, or subscribe, they'll automatically receive auto-responders for that pipeline and potentially become customers of that (and the up sells, down sells, profit maximizers, and cross sells that go with that.)

There are many strategies for structuring the loop back, but the return path Digital Marketer teaches in their "The Machine" product is one of the most powerful available. You can check it out yourself at http://glenkowalski.com/machine. As you know, I am a big fan of systems and processes, and The Machine breaks down what emails you should send when, so you can build your own automated follow up system.

Andrea Chaperones Auto-responder Magic is also amazing http://glenkowalski.com/arm, and will teach you how to write emails and strategies like a pro.

Best Practices

For immediately offered up sells and down sells, like when purchasing from a website, a good practice is to never offer more than two yes's and one no before finally delivering your product. You've probably purchased products where you have to click yes or no 10 times before you're finally taken to the product you tried to buy. By the time you get there you've probably forgotten what you bought.

When done correctly, when a customer buys something, endorphins are released, which act as a feel good drug. This makes the automatic up sell powerful because the "high" the client gets makes them want to keep on buying.

This boost in endorphins can be used for good or evil. So always treat your customer in the way you'd want to be treated. If you honestly believe your up sell is beneficial, then by all means offer it. But don't go taking advantage of the clients loose credit card to make sales they don't need or it will come back to bite you in the ass.

It feels sleazy on so many levels you'll want to think long and hard before you implement anything like it. Always keep in mind what's in your client's best interest. And don't be a sleazy online guru.

Surveys

We've mentioned surveys in earlier chapters for both lead magnets and education. But they also work well keeping existing clients engaged. When a client has completed your services or used your products, you should automatically send out a survey asking how you did.

This action alone might prompt further actions and sales if you provided good service.

Also, automated surveys may give you ideas about other services your existing clients would like to buy and you can sell them via your loop back mechanism.

Offer More

Whatever route you follow in your business, don't neglect your existing clients. No matter what service you offer, they're sure to need more, and you don't want them forgetting about you and going elsewhere. So don't forget about them.

Be a good steward and serve your leads in any way possible. Zig Ziglar said, "You can get anything you want in life if you help enough other people get what they want."

So help your clients get everything they want in life. If you do, they're sure to return again and again. And become advocates for your company and brand.

Action Steps

Action Step 1: Decide on an up sell offer for your primary service you've offered in the last chapters.

Action Step 2: If you sell your service online, setup an automatic up sell sequence in WooCommerce or other shopping cart to offer this up sell.

Action Step 3: Write a series of emails which keep your clients informed and engaged. Within that sequence, offer your up sell or other products and services they might be interested in. You must decide yourself whether it makes sense to send that email while you are still giving them your service, or if you trigger it after you've completed it.

Action Step 4: Setup an automation step that adds your client to your general newsletter or list.

There's an interesting psychological trait among humans where once someone has committed to something they will defend that position / commitment to everyone they talk with. This can be just as true with you and your brand as with their political affiliation. In the next chapter you'll discover how to tap into this trait and make win / win / win scenarios where your existing clients can become your biggest brand advocates and generate more leads and better conversions than any other marketing strategy you've ever used.

CHAPTER 18

Get Referrals

Now that you're attracting leads, converting them to customers, and knocking their socks off with professional automatic delivery systems, your customers are sure to become fans of your business.

So now is your chance to add the most powerful lead generation strategy you'll ever experience – referrals. By getting referrals, you're introducing new clients to the start of your temptation / attraction system. And better yet, building an unstoppable feedback loop, where more leads create more sales and then even more leads. But you're doing it with the advantage that a ton of credibility is already baked in to the process.

Which gives you more faith in a company's ability to service your needs?

An ad, on Facebook or local newspaper... Or a trusted friend and business associate recommending it to you?

I thought so...

In a moment, I'll tell you the biggest secret to getting all the referrals you could ever want, instantly. Then I'll tell you about how you can even automate that process. But first...

What would a stream of never ending referrals do for your business?

Imagine you have a system for attracting interested leads, converting them into customers, and making them raving fans of your services. So what if 1 in 4, or even 1 in 10, of those clients referred someone to your business? And what if they could get through that entire cycle in half the time?

Do you think that would make a significant difference to your bottom line?

If you run a local business, or you're a coach selling your books on Amazon, how valuable would it be if all of your customers left a review on Yelp, Amazon, or Barnes and Nobel telling everyone how amazing you are?

Are you getting excited yet? I hope so.

Do you want to know the secret for getting more referrals in your business? Here you go...

Ask for them.

Before you laugh, or shake your head and tell me how obvious that advice is, ask yourself if it's something you're doing on a regular and consistent basis. Because for most businesses, its not.

You're flying along, servicing your customers, collecting payments, figuring out new ways to generate leads and customers. If you're a coach or consultant, you're likely thinking about or writing a book or course. You've got speaking engagements, personal engagements, vacations, and more clouding up your day.

And even if you try to tell yourself to ask for referrals, you forget, 50%, 75%, or 99% of the time.

So why not automate the entire process?

Setup a campaign that's triggered when a service is fulfilled. This will vary with your business, but it could be based on a time delay after payment, after a certain number of emails, or any number of factors.

Send out an automatic email asking your client if they are happy with your services, and if they are, ask if they know anyone else you can help. You can then have them click a link in the email that takes them to a form where they can enter their friends name, phone number and email address.

Once that form is filled in, you can automatically create a task, assign it to a sales rep, and have that rep follow-up.

A word of warning here, DO NOT add this new prospect to a follow up list when following this approach - where your client enters the name and email. Sending an automated message sequence here will get you in trouble for spam.

There are certain steps that shouldn't be automated. This is one of them.

This approach requires a personal touch. It doesn't matter that the referral came from a friend. You MIGHT get away with one automatic email that mentioning the friends name and saying he recommended you. But I don't recommend it.

However, there are ways you can market to this referral automatically, but you have to get permission from the new lead first. I'll get into how to automate that approach in a minute. But it requires an extra step by the referrer, so you'll want to sweeten the pot for them a little first.

Automatic Referral Program

After you've delivered your services and wowed your customers, they will want to refer their friends. But everyone today is busy. They have their business or jobs, spouses and kids, hobbies and leisure, travel, and a million other things vying for each second of their time every day.

So tacking on one more item, like sending out an email or calling their friends, can often seem like too much.

To accumulate all the leads you want, you need to make the referral process as smooth as possible. And you also need to make sure it's a win / win / win for everyone involved. You do that with a real referral program. And since you are also busy with millions of other things, you do it with an automated referral program.

One that delivers value, and handles all the incentives, so you never have to lift a finger.

The first question you need to ask yourself, is what types of incentives would motivate your customers to take the step to endorse you to their friends and colleagues.

And the next is, how can you make it simple for them?

The answer to the first will depend on your business, relationships and goals. For many businesses, sending a gift is appropriate. For others, a small commission is a wiser choice. And for others, a graduated commission scale that increases as they give you more leads and referrals could create and alternative income stream for them. And a flood of new leads and customers for you.

You can have "Refer a Friend" programs. Or formal partner programs for partners who want to market for you while making an income stream.

Each choice is slightly more complicated to create, but all can be automated to cut manual work in the future.

How to Simplify the Process for Your Referrers

Collecting referrals who give you permission to market to them can be as simple as having your referrer give the new lead your phone number or email address. Then giving them an incentive them call you. This produces one of the strongest leads, but probably won't produce a high number.

A better approach would be having your past client send the new referral a link where they can fill out a form themselves which would opt them into your list.

You should also give your client / referral partner pre-written emails to forward to their friends and colleagues. Because it's coming from them, it's not considered spam, and the recipient has the opportunity to opt in or not.

Remember the recipient is more likely to "opt in" if the page they're redirected to is compelling and offers a compelling bribe.

Do you see how that works? Now we're creating the loop.

In sophisticated referral programs, you could give your referral partners marketing materials, pre-written email sequences, blog posts, banners and other advertisements, and more. This is more work and planning, but the power of these referral programs can skyrocket your revenues well beyond double, triple, or much more.

And again, once setup, the entire thing can be automated including motivational sequences you send directly to your referral partners to keep them engaged.

When you get to this level, you'll want to look closer at legalities of commissions (things like W-2's, etc.). And ensure partners ethical about spam and best practices.

A campaign like this would be started with an email asking if your past customer would like to be a referral partner and listing the benefits of the program. Since the client is already on your list, you tell them to click a link if they are interested, and automatically add them to your referral partner list.

That list would send a sequence of emails keeping them engaged and motivated while explaining more details about the program. It would then redirect partners to a page or a closed member's area on your site with banners, pre-written emails, affiliate links and other marketing material.

Each referral partner has a unique link to give to leads they are referring so that lead would be tracked and any future sales are credited to your referring partner.

And the magic is, it can happen on autopilot, bringing you leads while you hang out on a Caribbean island with a drink in your hand.

Product Launches and Events

One of the fastest ways to give your business a quick influx of cash is through a product launch, or re-launch. A service launch lends itself well to affiliate / referral promotions because it gives you the opportunity to create buzz and a sense of healthy competition among your referral partners.

Other events might be specials, webinars, or almost anything you can build a launch around.

Running an event like a launch though is a colossal undertaking. You have promotions to write, scripts to produce, emails, videos, landing pages, affiliate tracking, contest / point tracking, and more. You're sending mails to your prospective clients, and mails to your referral partners to keep them informed, engaged, and motivated.

Without the power of marketing automation, running a successful launch would be next to impossible. There are far too many moving parts to even consider such a monumental undertaking.

However, your marketing automation software allows you to spend the time out front, ahead of the promotion, to get everything setup before the craziness of the event kicks in. You'll be free to set up promotion campaigns for your own list, write emails for your partner's lists, and create videos or other marketing material before the launch begins.

You'll have a campaign for your partners, and another for your leads. Then, depending on your leads behavior, you'll route them down different paths in your pipeline, but all of this can be setup beforehand so it's ready to go.

Here's a quick run down of a very simple launch. It's easy to see why you'll want marketing automation setup to make this successful.

1. Send mail to referral partners hyping your launch, listing the benefits to the partners, and asking who would like to take part. Have them sign-up on a landing page if they do.

2. Send welcome mail to anyone who enrolls and a reminder mail to anyone who doesn't.

3. Kick off a motivational series of emails to your referrer partner with links to any promotional material you've created for them.

At this point, you can be hands off other than manually sending a daily broadcast mail with stats if you are making this a contest.

4. Create a sequence of emails for your own list promoting your launch. If you have multiple videos in your launch, send them a link to the first one.

5. Remind anyone in your list who hasn't watched the first video to watch it.

6. Promote the second video to everyone who has watched the first.

7. And so on throughout the launch.

As you are running your launch, several issues are bound to come up, and you need to be fully present to deal with those. So without automation there's no way you could send emails, tracking who has watched which videos, which referral partner is sending the most and best leads, etc. .

Automated marketing of your event is the key differentiator that'll differentiate between success and failure of your launch or other events.

Joint Ventures and Other Partnerships

A chapter on referrals would not be complete without at least mentioning one of the most powerful strategies for building your list of leads. Especially in the early days of your business.

That's working with other businesses owners in related, but non-competing marketing niches.

In the online marketing world, Joint Venture partnerships work like a 2-way referral program. While the details of Joint Ventures vary from deal to deal, you're essentially making an agreement with another business owner to promote your business to his or her list. Then, agreeing to refer others back.

With this business arrangement, you are both exposing your product or service to a brand new set of eyes. They're an excellent way to build your list and generate a large amount of interest in your business in a short amount of time.

Partnerships like this seem like lots of effort. But with automation, the process almost manages itself. You must create a campaign with a series of emails for your partner, and that's really it for their side. For your side, you'll need tracking links and a dedicated landing page. You'll then want to create a special follow-up series, particularly aimed at your partner's niche since you know where these people are coming from.

In most cases, you'll want to provide the email copy to your partner so they can feed it into their Auto-responder series or marketing automation software. But that's it. At that point, your new leads are plugged into the attraction system you've already built. But now, they're preconditioned to convert, because someone they already know, like, and trust has referred them. This makes these leads a spectacular business builder because you have someone else vouching for your authenticity, building your credibility.

Action Steps

Action Step 1: Brainstorm several ideas for incentives you can offer your past customers so they'll become bigger referrers to your business.

Action Step 2: Setup your referral tracking system.

Action Step 3: Reach out to past clients and ask if they know anyone they can send in your direction for a free consult or to request more information.

Action Step 4: Reach out to 3 potential Joint Venture Partners. Preferably, people in your industry but not competing businesses. Preferably this would be a business owner you already know and are comfortable talking to. Ask them if they'll send a promotional email to their list, if you do the same and / or pay them a commission on any closed deals.

CHAPTER 19

Now, Get Out There and Do It

Automating and systematizing your business will transform your income and free time by leveraging your knowledge and skills. You'll be free to pursue the parts of your business you enjoy and make the most impact. Rather than repeating the same processes until you can't take it any more. Or worse yet, performing different tasks and processes and reinventing the wheel every time because you don't have a system or process to follow.

Most business owners are so busy running around chasing tasks that are easily automated, they're missing out on the opportunities to create impact and grow the business the way they want. By doing this, they lose the ability to serve their clients to the best of your abilities.

By not automating your marketing, you're not only leaving money on the table, and losing your free time (and mind), you're also performing a disservice to your existing clients.

If you follow the action steps outlined in this book, you will have more leads, more sales, more referrals, and much more free time because of it. But it will only happen if you put the steps you've learned into action.

You're busy. You know that, and I know that. But if you're waiting for the right time to implement this system and the automation behind running it, you'll never get there. Tomorrow never comes. If you haven't started already, go right now to http://glenkowalski.com/activecampaign and request your 14-day free trial right now. Just taking that action step will get you on the road to bigger things, and won't cost you a penny.

Start small. Get your system in place, add your sales pipeline, and then gradually add your temptation, amplification, loop back and referral systems. Each step will have a profound impact on your business. But when combined, you will notice a monumental shift in your business. I didn't write this book to give you a small increase although a tiny increase will no doubt be a large return on investment. I wrote it for you to make a massive shift. More free time, higher revenues, and most importantly the ability to make a large impact on the success of your clients. In whatever business you operate.

More Help

If you're looking for a more detailed class on the specifics of automation, you can get one on my website at http://glenkowalski.com/automation-course. This course will walk you through every aspect of automation, not from the system perspective as taught in this book, but in the specific tasks.

That course is written to apply to your business whether you are using ActiveCampaign, Infusionsoft, ActOn, Marketo or other automation solution. The nitty-gritty of the steps might change from one version to another, but the course applies to all of them.

If you'd like to learn the exact steps for generating all the leads you can handle on autopilot, visit http://glenkowalski.com/webcast

The important thing is starting right now. If you'd like to talk to a real person about your goals and plans, enroll for a free "Double Your Revenue Breakout Session" right now at http://glenkowalski.com/consultation-request and we'll chat on Skype for an hour free to get clarity on your specific business and whether marketing automation is right for you.

Or, if you're looking for a speaker at your event, or to talk to your team, I'm available for select speaking engagements and person-to-person interviews. Just email me at glen@glenkowalski.com and we'll make the arrangements.

I hope you enjoyed reading this book; I've enjoyed writing it for you. But more importantly, I look forward to hearing your massive success stories as you implement these systems in your own business.

As a reader, I'd love to offer you a free road map, built specifically for your business, please visit http://glenkowalski.com/consultation-request

Skyrocket your revenue this year by systemizing and automating your business, leveraging your time and by being unconventional. And above all else, think different; I look forward to seeing you and hearing your stories down the unconventional road.

ABOUT THE AUTHOR

Glen Kowalski, founder of Palm Tree Marketing Group Ltd., is an Unconventional Entrepreneur. He is driven to help non-conformists' committed to taking action and responsibility over their own lives; Including the freedom seekers who never want to be reliant on government, a boss, or anyone else to dictate how or where they live their lives or run their businesses.

Glen helps his clients, independence-seeking entrepreneurs, create online Sales, Marketing, and Webcast Automation. Primarily, this includes service professionals like coaches, consultants, experts, and speakers, and those in non-mainstream fields. His mission is awakening people to the availability of personal, location, business, and financial independence and serving those who are drawn to the unconventional.

www.ingramcontent.com/pod-product-compliance
Lightning Source LLC
Chambersburg PA
CBHW070224210526
45169CB00023B/194